PLAYS FOR PERFORMANCE

A series designed for
contemporary production and study
Edited by
Nicholas Rudall and Bernard Sahlins

HENRIK IBSEN

The Master Builder

In a New Translation by
Nicholas Rudall

Ivan R. Dee
CHICAGO

Library of Congress Cataloging-in-Publication Data:
Ibsen, Henrik, 1828–1906.
  [Bygmester Solness. English]
  The master builder / Henrik Ibsen : in a new translation by Nicholas Rudall.
      p.   cm. — (Plays for performance)
    ISBN 1-56663-043-6. — ISBN 1-56663-042-8 (paper)
    I. Rudall, Nicholas. II. Title. III. Series.
  PT8859.A38 1994
  839.8'226—dc20   93-44686

INTRODUCTION
by Nicholas Rudall

This version of *The Master Builder* is, as all the other plays in this series, translated and adapted with performance in mind. The play itself is often deeply symbolic, but the language is rigorously naturalistic. My goal is to make it eminently speakable. As in my previous Ibsen translations, I have replaced long periodic sentences with the shorter rhythms of spoken, as opposed to written, English.

Some observations on the text and the stage settings:

Although the play and the characters are riddled with pain and anguish, the *pace* of the writing is often extremely light and rapid. In fact there is a great deal of humor in the play. And this humor comes from the quickness of mind of Solness and Hilde in particular. Many of the short phrases or single words in the interchanges are meant to be delivered rapidly. For example, the following sequence illustrates the need for the actor to eschew the ponderous and embrace lightness.

SOLNESS: And what on earth did I do next?

HILDE: Well, this is really the limit! You've forgotten that too! How could anyone forget a thing like that.

SOLNESS: All right, just a hint...could you give me just a—

3

HILDE: *(looking intently at him)* You took me in your arms and you kissed me, Mr. Solness.

SOLNESS: I did? *(getting up open-mouthed)*

HILDE: Oh yes. You did. You held me in your arms. Both arms. You bent me backwards and you kissed me. Many times.

SOLNESS: But my dear Miss Wangel...

HILDE: *(rising)* You're not going to deny it?

SOLNESS: Yes. I am. I absolutely deny it.

HILDE: *(looking scornfully at him)* I see. *(She turns and walks to the stove. Stands motionless, her back to him. Hands behind her back. Short pause.)*

I have provided Ibsen's setting only for Act I—intentionally. The play can be accommodated by this single setting. Act Two is normally set in the drawing room of Solness's house. Act Three is set on the veranda.

CHARACTERS

HALVARD SOLNESS, the Master Builder
ALINE SOLNESS, his wife
DOCTOR HERDAL, the family doctor
KNUT BROVIK, a former architect now employed by
  Solness
RAGNAR BROVIK, Knut's son
KAJA FOSLI, Solness's bookkeeper
MISS HILDE WANGEL

The play can be performed with this number of actors. Ibsen calls for "Some Ladies" and "A crowd in the garden." These can be effectively represented by offstage speech and noise in Act Three.

This translation was first performed in 1986 at Court Theatre, the professional theatre at the University of Chicago.

The Master Builder

ACT 1

A plainly furnished workroom in Solness's house. Folding doors in the wall to the left lead to the entryway. To the right is a door to the inner rooms. Downstage left, a desk with books, papers, and writing materials. Upstage, beyond the folding doors, a stove. In the right-hand corner, a sofa with a table and a couple of chairs. On the table, a carafe of water and a glass. A smaller table with a rocker and an armchair in the right foreground. Lights for working lit over the drafting room table, on the table in the corner, and on the desk.

In the drafting room Knut Brovik and his son Ragnar are sitting, busy with blueprints and calculations. Knut is a gaunt old man with white hair and beard. He wears a rather threadbare but well-preserved black coat, glasses, and a white muffler somewhat yellowed by age. Ragnar Brovik is in his thirties, well-dressed, blond, with a slight stoop. Kaja Fosli stands at a desk in the front room, writing in a ledger. She is a delicate young girl of twenty some years, trimly dressed but rather sickly in appearance. She is wearing a green eyeshade. All three work on for a time in silence.

KNUT BROVIK: *(suddenly stands up from the table as if in distress; breathes heavily and laboriously as he comes forward)* No! I can't go on much longer.

KAJA: *(coming to him)* Aren't you feeling well, uncle? Is it worse tonight?

9

BROVIK: It gets worse every day.

RAGNAR: *(has risen and come to them)* You had better go home, father. Try to get a bit of sleep.

BROVIK: *(impatiently)* You want me in bed? You want me to suffocate and die? Is that it?

KAJA: Then take a little walk.

RAGNAR: Yes, do. I'll come with you.

BROVIK: *(angrily)* I won't go till he comes back. I'm going to do it tonight. I'm going to have it out with... *(resentfully)* with him—with our "master."

KAJA: *(upset)* Oh no, uncle. Please! It can wait!

RAGNAR: Yes, father. Not yet.

BROVIK: *(breathing heavily)* Ha! Not yet! How much time have I got left?

KAJA: *(listening)* Sh! I think I hear him on the stairs.

(they return to work... brief silence)

(Halvard Solness enters from the entry hall. He is a middle-aged man, strong and forceful, with close-cropped, curly hair, a dark mustache, and thick, dark eyebrows. His jacket, grey-green with wide lapels, is buttoned with the collar turned up. On his head is a soft grey felt hat, and under his arm a couple of portfolios.)

SOLNESS: *(by the door, pointing to inner room, whispers)* Are they gone?

KAJA: *(quietly, shaking her head)* No.

(She takes the shade off her eyes. Solness crosses the room, throws his hat on a chair and the portfolios on the table by the sofa, and goes to the desk. Kaja keeps on writing, nervous and uneasy.)

SOLNESS: What's that you're writing, Miss Fosli? Let me see it please, Miss Fosli—*(leans over, pretending to examine the ledger, whispers)* Kaja?

KAJA: *(softly while still writing)* Yes?

SOLNESS: Why do you always take your eyeshade off when I come in?

KAJA: I look so awful with it on.

SOLNESS: *(smiling)* And of course you can't bear the thought of looking—

KAJA: No, I can't. Especially when *you* are here looking at me.

SOLNESS: *(stroking her hair)* My dear Kaja...

KAJA: *(averting her head)* Hush—they can hear you.

(Solness crosses the room, casually, and pauses at the door)

SOLNESS: Did anyone come to see me—while I was out?

RAGNAR: Yes, yes, that young couple—the one who want a villa built out at Lovstrand.

SOLNESS: Oh them! Well, they'll have to wait. I have no plans, no ideas yet.

RAGNAR: *(coming forward, hesitantly)* They really wanted the drawings as soon as possible.

SOLNESS: Of course—they all do.

BROVIK: *(looking up)* What they said was that they couldn't wait to have a house built of their own.

SOLNESS: Yes, yes, it's always the same. So people take whatever's given them. What do they get? A roof over their heads—an address. But nothing that could be called a home. No, no thank you. They can find somebody else. Tell them *that* the next time they come.

BROVIK: *(pushing glasses onto forehead and looking at him in amazement)* Somebody else? You'd turn down the commission?

SOLNESS: Yes. Yes. Damn it. If that's what has to happen, yes. I'd rather do that than just throw something together. *(angrily)* Besides, I know nothing about these people.

BROVIK: They're good people, reliable...ask Ragnar. He's a friend of the family, very reliable.

SOLNESS: Reliable! That's not what I mean. Good Lord—don't you understand me either? *(sharply)* Look—I don't *know* these people. I will have nothing to do with them. They can find someone else. I don't care.

BROVIK: *(rising)* Do you really mean that?

SOLNESS: *(sullen)* Yes, I do. For once. *(crosses room)*

(Brovik glances at Ragnar. Ragnar makes a warning gesture. Brovik crosses to Solness.)

BROVIK: May I have a word with you?

SOLNESS: Of course.

BROVIK: Kaja, go inside for a minute.

KAJA: *(uneasily)* Uncle—please.

BROVIK: Do as I say, child. Shut the door after you.

(Kaja goes into other room, glances at Solness with a pleading look.)

BROVIK: *(quietly)* I don't want the children to know how really sick I am.

12

SOLNESS: Yes, you've been looking so very frail these last weeks.

BROVIK: It'll be over soon. I have less and less strength each day.

SOLNESS: Have a seat. Rest a moment.

BROVIK: Thank you, may I?

SOLNESS: *(placing a chair)* Here. There we are. Now?

BROVIK: Yes, well, it's Ragnar. I can't get him out of my mind. What is going to happen?

SOLNESS: Well, of course, your son can stay on with me for as long as he likes. Naturally.

BROVIK: But that's just it. He doesn't like. He feels...he feels that he must leave.

SOLNESS: Well, my first reaction is that he is very well paid—but if he is after a small raise, I wouldn't be averse to...

BROVIK: No. No. It's not that. *(impatiently)* Look, sooner or later he must have the chance to work on his own.

SOLNESS: *(avoiding Brovik's eyes)* Do you think Ragnar has enough talent for that?

BROVIK: That is what is tearing me apart—I'm beginning to have my doubts about him. You see, you've never, ever given him a word of encouragement. And yet I can't help thinking that I'm wrong. He must have the talent.

SOLNESS: But he has learned nothing—nothing thoroughly anyway. Except, of course, he's a competent draftsman.

BROVIK: *(looking at him—hatred concealed...hoarse voice)* When you worked for me, you learned nothing. But that didn't stop you. You got ahead, pushed ahead. You walked all over me and anyone else who got in your way.

SOLNESS: Let me say that luck was on my side.

BROVIK: Yes. True. Everything was on your side. But how can you just let me go to my grave without seeing what my son can do? *(pause)* And before I go, I want to see them married.

SOLNESS: *(sharply)* Is that what she wants?

BROVIK: Kaja, not so much. But Ragnar doesn't let a day go by without talking about it. *(pleading)* You must! You have to help him get some freelance work. Something! I must see *something* that my boy has done. Do you hear me!

SOLNESS: *(angrily)* Damn it! Do you think I can just—do you think commissions grow on trees?

BROVIK: He could have one now. An excellent commission. An important piece of work.

SOLNESS: *(surprised, troubled)* He could?

BROVIK: If you'd give permission.

SOLNESS: What do you mean?

BROVIK: He could build the house at Lovstrand.

SOLNESS: No. That is mine. I shall build that house.

BROVIK: I thought you weren't interested in it anymore.

SOLNESS: Not interested? Me? Who says so?

BROVIK: You said so yourself. A few minutes ago.

SOLNESS: Don't listen to what I *say*. . . . Would they give Ragnar the commission?

14

BROVIK: Yes. All you'd have to do is look them over, give your approval and then...

SOLNESS: Then they'd have Ragnar build their house.

BROVIK: They like his designs, his ideas. They thought it was very unusual—different. That's what they said.

SOLNESS: Ah. "New." "Modern." Not the old-fashioned stuff that I build.

BROVIK: They thought it was...different, that's all.

SOLNESS: *(bitterly)* They came here and talked with Ragnar while I was out.

BROVIK: They came to see you. They wanted to ask if you'd give up the...

SOLNESS: *(explosively)* Give up? I...

BROVIK: That is, if you found Ragnar's plans to your...

SOLNESS: Give up? I should just hand over to your son?!

BROVIK: Give up the commission, that's all they meant.

SOLNESS: It's the same thing. *(wry laugh)* God. Halvard Solness...it's time for you to retire. Give up. Step aside! For the younger generation. Youngest. Step aside. Make room.

BROVIK: Good Lord...there's room enough—room for more than one man....

SOLNESS: There is not. Not here. Not anymore. But...well...never mind. Look, I'm not giving up. I do not step aside. Not for anyone. Certainly not of my own free will. Never.

BROVIK: *(rising with some effort)* And what about me? Must I leave this world without any hope, any final moment of happiness? Without any faith, any belief in my son? Without seeing one single example of what he can do? Is that what you want?

SOLNESS: *(turning away, half whispers)* Don't ask any more of me. Not now.

BROVIK: Yes. Now. Answer me. Is that how you want me to go to my grave?

SOLNESS: *(after struggling inwardly, he speaks in a low but firm voice)* You will have to face death in the best way you can.

BROVIK: Then that's it. *(he walks away)*

SOLNESS: *(follows him, almost desperately)* Can't you see? What else can I do? That's the way I am. I can't change.

BROVIK: No. No. I suppose you can't. *(falters, holds on to back of sofa)* May I have a glass of water?

SOLNESS: *(pouring)* Here you are.

BROVIK: *(drinks, sets down glass)* Thank you.

SOLNESS: *(opening door)* Ragnar—come. Take your father home.

(Ragnar gets up quickly. He and Kaja come into the workroom.)

RAGNAR: Father—what's the matter?

BROVIK: Give me your arm. We'll go home.

RAGNAR: All right. Get your things, Kaja.

SOLNESS: Miss Fosli will have to stay for a little longer. I have to write a letter.

16

BROVIK: Good night. Sleep well, if you can.

SOLNESS: Good night.

(Brovik and Ragnar leave. Kaja moves to the desk. Solness stands, head lowered.)

KAJA: *(hesitantly)* Is there a letter?

SOLNESS: *(curtly)* Of course not. *(fierce look)* Kaja!

KAJA: *(frightened; quiet voice)* Yes?

SOLNESS: Come closer.

KAJA: What do you want?

SOLNESS: Is this your idea? *(looking at her)*

KAJA: No. No. That's not true.

SOLNESS: But the marriage—is that what you want?

KAJA: *(quietly)* Ragnar and I have been engaged for about five years—and so...

SOLNESS: And so? You think it can't go on forever? Is that it?

KAJA: Ragnar and my uncle tell me I must—and so I think I will have to.

SOLNESS: *(moves gently)* You care for him though, don't you—a little.

KAJA: I cared for Ragnar very much—once, before I came here to work for you.

SOLNESS: And now? Don't you care at all?

KAJA: *(reaching for him passionately)* Oh, you know that I care only for one, for one man only. Nobody else in the whole world. I'll never care for anyone else.

SOLNESS: Yes. It's easy to talk. Then you desert me. Leave me to cope with everything myself.

KAJA: But couldn't I stay on here with you, even if Ragnar were to...

SOLNESS: No. No. That's out of the question. If Ragnar goes into business for himself, he will need you.

KAJA: I don't see how I could ever leave you. *(wringing her hands nervously)* It's impossible.

SOLNESS: Then get these stupid ideas out of Ragnar's head. Marry him, marry him ten times over. *(changing his tone)* Look, don't let him lose a good job here with me. If he stays, then you can stay too, here with me. Kaja, my dear child.

KAJA: Oh God. How I would love that. If only we could do that.

SOLNESS: *(stroking her head with both hands and whispering to her)* I can't be without you. Do you understand? I can't. I've got to have you close to me. Every day.

KAJA: *(quaking with excitement)* Oh God. God.

SOLNESS: *(kisses her hair)* Kaja. Kaja.

KAJA: *(sinks down before him)* Oh how good you are to me. How unbelievably good to me.

SOLNESS: *(intensely)* Get up. Quick. Someone's coming.

(He helps her up. She staggers over to the desk. Mrs. Solness enters. She looks thin, nervous, though her former beauty still shows. Blonde ringlets. Dressed stylishly, entirely in black. Speaks slowly, sadly.)

MRS. SOLNESS: *(in doorway)* Halvard!

SOLNESS: *(turning)* Ah—it's you my dear.

MRS. SOLNESS: *(glances at Kaja)* Am I interrupting?

SOLNESS: Not at all. Miss Fosli has just one short letter to write.

MRS. SOLNESS: Yes. So I see.

SOLNESS: Did you want me for something, Aline?

MRS. SOLNESS: I just wanted to tell you that Dr. Herdal is in the living room. Perhaps you could join us.

SOLNESS: (*looking at her*) Hmm...is it urgent?

MRS. SOLNESS: No, not urgent. He stopped by to see me but I'm sure he'd like to say hello to you too.

SOLNESS: (*laughing to himself*) Yes, I'm sure he would. Well—you'd better ask him to wait a little.

MRS. SOLNESS: You'll join us later?

SOLNESS: Possibly. In a while. In a while. Later, my dear.

MRS. SOLNESS: (*glancing at Kaja*) Now don't forget, Halvard. (leaves, closes door)

KAJA: (*softly*) Oh my God—she must think I'm awful.

SOLNESS: No. Not in the least. It's the same as always. But you'd better go now, Kaja.

KAJA: Yes. I must go.

SOLNESS: (*firmly*) And you'll take care of what we talked about. You understand?

KAJA: If it were only up to me...

SOLNESS: I want it taken care of. By tomorrow...at the latest.

KAJA: (*frightened*) If it doesn't work out, I'll be prepared to break off the engagement.

19

SOLNESS: *(angry)* Break it off? Are you mad? You'd break it off?

KAJA: *(in despair)* Yes, if necessary. I have to—I must stay here with you. I can't leave you. That would be impossible.

SOLNESS: *(explosively)* But God damn it! What about Ragnar? It's Ragnar that...

KAJA: *(looks at him terrified)* Is it only because of Ragnar that—that you...

SOLNESS: *(collecting himself)* No. No of course not. You don't understand me, either. *(gently, softly)* It's you that I need. You more than anything, Kaja. But that is why you must make Ragnar keep his job. There, there, you must go home now.

KAJA: Yes. Good night then.

SOLNESS: Good night. *(as she is leaving)* Wait a moment! Are Ragnar's drawings in there?

KAJA: I don't think he took them with him.

SOLNESS: See if you can find them for me, would you? I might take a look at them.

KAJA: *(happy)* Would you? Oh please do.

SOLNESS: Just for you, Kaja. Just for you. Now would you get them right away?

(She hurries to the table, opens the drawer and finds portfolio, returns)

KAJA: I think they're all here.

SOLNESS: Good. Put them on the table for me.

KAJA: Good night then. *(looking)* Please think well of me.

SOLNESS: Oh, that I always do. Good night, my sweet Kaja. *(glances right)* Go. Go now.

(Mrs. Solness and Dr. Herdal enter. He is stoutish, elderly. Round, good-humored face, clean-shaven. Thin, blond hair. Wears gold spectacles.)

MRS. SOLNESS: *(in doorway)* Halvard, the doctor can't wait any longer.

SOLNESS: Well—why don't you come in?

MRS. SOLNESS: *(to Kaja who is turning down the lamp)* Have you finished the letter already, Miss Fosli?

KAJA: *(in confusion)* The letter?

SOLNESS: Yes. It was a short one.

MRS. SOLNESS: I'm sure it was.

SOLNESS: You may go now, Miss Fosli. Please be on time in the morning.

KAJA: I will, sir. Good night, Mrs. Solness. *(she leaves)*

MRS. SOLNESS: You're lucky to have her, Halvard— your Miss Fosli.

SOLNESS: Indeed. She's very capable. In all sorts of ways.

MRS. SOLNESS: So it seems.

DR. HERDAL: Good bookkeeper?

SOLNESS: Well, she's had a lot of experience these past two years. She's such a nice person. Thoughtful. Obliging.

MRS. SOLNESS: That must be a comfort.

SOLNESS: Yes. It is. Especially when you're not used to it.

MRS. SOLNESS: *(demonstrating)* How can you say that, Halvard?

SOLNESS: No. My dear, Aline. No. No. I beg your pardon.

MRS. SOLNESS: It was nothing. Well then, doctor, you'll stop by later and have a cup of tea.

DR. HERDAL: I have to make one house call and then I'll come back.

MRS. SOLNESS: Thank you. *(she leaves)*

SOLNESS: Are you in a hurry, doctor?

DR. HERDAL: No, not at all.

SOLNESS: May I speak with you for a moment?

DR. HERDAL: By all means.

SOLNESS: Then let's sit down. *(motions Dr. Herdal to rocking chair and sits in arm chair; looks into his eyes)* Tell me, did you notice anything odd about Aline.

DR. HERDAL: You mean now? When she was here?

SOLNESS: Yes. The way she acted towards me. Did you notice anything?

DR. HERDAL: *(smiling)* Well—umm—one could hardly help noticing—that your wife...

SOLNESS: Go on.

DR. HERDAL: That your wife isn't particularly fond of Miss Fosli.

SOLNESS: Nothing more? I've noticed that myself.

DR. HERDAL: It's not surprising.

SOLNESS: Why do you say that?

DR. HERDAL: It's not surprising that she wouldn't exactly approve of your seeing so much of another woman. Day in, day out.

SOLNESS: I suppose you're right. I suppose Aline is right. But it can't be helped.

DR. HERDAL: Couldn't you hire a man instead?

SOLNESS: Someone off the street? No thank you. That would never do for me.

DR. HERDAL: But if your wife—she's not well, you know. This could be too much for her.

SOLNESS: I told you—it can't be helped. Kaja Fosli is indispensable. No one else will do.

DR. HERDAL: No one?

SOLNESS: *(curtly)* No one.

DR. HERDAL: *(moving his chair closer)* Now listen to me, Mr. Solness. May I ask you a question? Just between ourselves?

SOLNESS: By all means.

DR. HERDAL: Well. Women, you know, women sense these things—intuition—ummm...

SOLNESS: That's true. Very true, but...

DR. HERDAL: Well—well, if your wife can't endure this Kaja Fosli—

SOLNESS: Well, what then?

DR. HERDAL: Doesn't she have grounds—however slight—for not liking her?

SOLNESS: *(rising)* Ah...

DR. HERDAL: Now don't take offense. Doesn't she?

SOLNESS: *(curt but decisive)* No.

23

DR. HERDAL: None at all?

SOLNESS: None at all. Except her own suspicious mind.

DR. HERDAL: Look. I realize that you've known a good many women in your time.

SOLNESS: Yes, I have.

DR. HERDAL: And you've been attracted to many of them, too.

SOLNESS: Yes. That is true.

DR. HERDAL: But in this instance—there is nothing like that?

SOLNESS: No. Nothing whatever—on my part.

DR. HERDAL: But on hers?

SOLNESS: I don't think you have the right to ask that question, doctor.

DR. HERDAL: We were discussing your wife's intuition.

SOLNESS: We were, yes. And in fact— *(lowering his voice)* Aline's intuition, as you call it, has sometimes been justified.

DR. HERDAL: I thought it might.

SOLNESS: Dr. Herdal, let me tell you a story—a strange one. That is, if you'd care to hear.

DR. HERDAL: I enjoy a good story.

SOLNESS: Good. Well then. I'm sure you remember how I took on Knut Brovik and his son? That was when things were going badly for the old man.

DR. HERDAL: I vaguely remember. Yes.

SOLNESS: Well. Anyway. They're really quite clever, those two. In their own way. They have ability. But the son decided to get engaged. He was all for getting married—for starting his own career as an architect. The young people today—that's how they are. That's all they think of.

DR. HERDAL: *(laughing)* Yes. It's a terrible habit—this marital coupling.

SOLNESS: Yes, but that can't interfere with my work. I need Ragnar. Here. I need the old man too. He's very good on stress calculation—cubic content—all the darned detailed work.

DR. HERDAL: Of course, that's important.

SOLNESS: It is. But Ragnar felt that he had to branch out on his own. There was no reasoning with him.

DR. HERDAL: Nonetheless he's still with you.

SOLNESS: Yes. But here's the interesting part. One day she came in here—Kaja Fosli—she was doing some errand for them. Never been here before. And when I saw them together, saw how infatuated they were with each other, then the thought struck me: if I could get her to work here in the office, perhaps Ragnar would stay on too.

DR. HERDAL: Reasonable enough.

SOLNESS: But I didn't say a word—then—just stood looking at her, wishing in every fiber of my being that I had her here. I chatted for a few minutes. Very friendly. Then she left.

DR. HERDAL: So?

SOLNESS: The next day, late in the evening, after Brovik and Ragnar had gone home, she came by to see me. She behaved as if we had already struck an agreement.

DR. HERDAL: What kind of agreement?

SOLNESS: Exactly what I'd been wishing for the previous day. Even though I'd not said a word.

DR. HERDAL: That *is* strange.

SOLNESS: I told you. She wanted to know what her duties would be, would she start the following morning. Things like that.

DR. HERDAL: Wasn't that simply to be with her fiancé, don't you think?

SOLNESS: Yes, that was my first impression. But no, that was not it. From the moment she started work, she seemed to—to drift away from him.

DR. HERDAL: And over to you?

SOLNESS: Yes. Completely. If I look at her when her back is turned, I can tell she feels it. She trembles, quivers when I come near her. How do you explain that, Dr. Herdal?

DR. HERDAL: Oh, it's not so difficult.

SOLNESS: Well . . . but all the rest of it. The fact that she believed that I had actually told her things that were only in my mind. My silent thoughts. What do you say about that? How do you explain that?

DR. HERDAL: I wouldn't try to.

SOLNESS: No. I thought so. That's why I've never been able to discuss it until now. But you see, the longer it goes on, the more of a damned nuisance it becomes. Here, day in day out I have to pretend that I'm—and it's not fair to her, poor girl. *(angrily)* But it's not my fault! And if she leaves, Ragnar will go too.

DR. HERDAL: And you've said nothing of this to your wife?

SOLNESS: No.

DR. HERDAL: Why not, for God's sake?

SOLNESS: *(looking at him intently)* Because somehow I feel that a self-inflicted wound is justified. It is right for Aline to be wrong about me.

DR. HERDAL: I don't understand what you're saying.

SOLNESS: Yes. Don't you see—it's like making a small payment on some immense, incalculable debt.

DR. HERDAL: To your wife?

SOLNESS: Yes. It eases the mind. You can breathe more freely. For a while.

DR. HERDAL: I really, God help me, *don't* understand—

SOLNESS: *(interrupting and rising)* Well—we'll not speak of it again. *(crosses room, returns, smiles at the doctor)* Well, I'm sure you feel you've done an excellent job of drawing me out—hmm?

DR. HERDAL: Drawing you out? I still don't understand what you've been saying.

SOLNESS: Oh come now. Tell me the truth. It's so clear, so obvious to me.

DR. HERDAL: What's so obvious?

SOLNESS: That behind this mask of affability, you're watching me carefully.

DR. HERDAL: What on earth makes you think that?

SOLNESS: Because you think that I'm— *(explosively)* oh damn it—you think the same about me as Aline does.

DR. HERDAL: What does she think?

SOLNESS: She—she's beginning to believe that I'm— that I'm ill.

DR. HERDAL: Ill? You? No, she's never said a word. What do you think is the matter with you?

SOLNESS: *(leaning forward, quietly)* Aline believes that I'm losing my mind. That is what she thinks.

DR. HERDAL: *(rising)* My dear Solness—

SOLNESS: I swear to you that she does. And she has begun to convince you too. Oh, I tell you, doctor—I can see it in your face. It's so clear. I'm not a fool. I'm not, I can tell you that.

DR. HERDAL: Look, I'm telling you—

SOLNESS: *(interrupting)* All right, all right—let's drop the subject. Private worlds. *(quiet amusement)* But now, doctor, will you listen to me a moment—

DR. HERDAL: Yes.

SOLNESS: If you don't think that I'm—that I'm ill—or mad, deranged, that sort of thing— then—

DR. HERDAL: Then what?

SOLNESS: Then you must imagine that I'm a very happy man.

DR. HERDAL: Is that imaginary?

SOLNESS: *(with a wry laugh)* Oh no, not at all. God forbid. Just think...to be Solness...the master builder. Halvard Solness! Thank you, my friend.

DR. HERDAL: Well, to some extent it's true. You have been extraordinarily lucky in a way.

SOLNESS: *(thin smile)* Yes. Yes I have. Can't complain about that.

DR. HERDAL: In a strange way it started with the fire. When that monstrosity burned down! That was a stroke of luck.

SOLNESS: It was my wife's house, remember? The family home.

DR. HERDAL: Yes, it was a tragedy for her.

SOLNESS: She's never recovered really. Not after twelve, thirteen years.

DR. HERDAL: It was what happened after...that must have been the worst.

SOLNESS: The two together.

DR. HERDAL: But you yourself...you rose from those ashes. You were just a poor boy from the country...and now you are—indeed—at the top of your profession. Yes, Solness. You have had luck on your side.

SOLNESS: But that's why I'm so desperately afraid.

DR. HERDAL: Afraid? Afraid of having luck on your side?

SOLNESS: It torments me—day and night. Because it can't last. It can't.

DR. HERDAL: Nonsense! What's going to change? What could change it?

SOLNESS: Youth.

DR. HERDAL: Ha, youth! You're not finished yet. You're in your prime. Never better.

SOLNESS: There will be a change. I can feel it coming. Someone will come. Soon. Someone will come and say, "Move over. Step aside." And the world will follow...shaking their fists and screaming, "Make room, make room, make room!" Yes, doctor, you'd better watch out. Someday soon, youth will come knocking on the door.

DR. HERDAL: And what is so bad about that?

(knock on the door)

SOLNESS: What was that? Did you hear something?

DR. HERDAL: Someone knocking.

SOLNESS: Come in!

(Hilde Wangel enters from the hall. Medium height, lithe and physically attractive, slightly suntanned. She wears hiking clothes, a short skirt, a sailor blouse open at the neck, a little sailor hat. She has a knapsack on her back, a wool plaid with a strap, and a long alpenstock. She crosses directly to Solness, eyes shining and happy.)

HILDE: Good evening.

SOLNESS: *(uncertainly)* Good evening.

HILDE: *(laughing)* I don't think you recognize me.

SOLNESS: No...as a matter of fact I...at the moment...

DR. HERDAL: *(coming to her)* Ah, but I do. Miss...

HILDE: *(delighted)* Oh no! Is it you?...I was...

DR. HERDAL: It certainly is. *(to Solness)* We met last summer. At one of the lodges in the mountains. *(to Hilde)* What happened to all the other young ladies?

HILDE: Oh, they left. They went off to the west slope.

DR. HERDAL: They didn't enjoy our somewhat noisy evenings?

HILDE: No. They certainly did not.

DR. HERDAL: *(wagging his finger)* Anyway, you seemed to enjoy yourself... you can't say you didn't flirt with us on occasion.

HILDE: It was more fun than knitting socks with all the old ladies.

DR. HERDAL: *(laughing)* Couldn't agree with you more.

SOLNESS: Did you just arrive in town?

HILDE: Yes. Just a few moments ago.

DR. HERDAL: All by yourself, Miss Wangel?

HILDE: Of course.

SOLNESS: Wangel? Is your name Wangel?

HILDE: *(looking at him with a smile of amusement)* Yes, that's my name.

SOLNESS: Are you the daughter of the commissioner of public health up at Lysanger.

HILDE: *(still amused)* Yes. I have no other father.

SOLNESS: Ah... no, that's where we met. Up at Lysanger. When I built the towers for the church that summer.

HILDE: *(eyes fixed on him)* It's ten years to the day. Exactly.

SOLNESS: You couldn't have been more than a child then.

HILDE: *(carelessly)* I was about thirteen.

DR. HERDAL: Is this your first visit here, Miss Wangel?

HILDE: Yes, it is.

SOLNESS: Then you don't know anyone in town.

HILDE: No one—except you. And your wife, of course.

SOLNESS: You know my wife?

HILDE: Just slightly. We met up in the mountains. At the resort.

SOLNESS: Ah. I see.

HILDE: She told me to come and visit her if ever I came into town. *(smile)* Not that I expected it.

SOLNESS: I'm surprised she never mentioned it to me—

(Hilde puts down the alpenstock by the stove, takes off her knapsack, and puts it and the plaid on the sofa. Dr. Herdal offers to help. Solness stands, looking at her.)

(Hilde crosses to Solness)

HILDE: Could you put me up for the night?

SOLNESS: I'm sure that can be arranged.

HILDE: I haven't got any other clothes—apart from the ones on my back. There's some underthings in my knapsack, but they need to be washed. They're filthy.

SOLNESS: Well, I'm sure we can arrange that too. Just let me call my wife—

DR. HERDAL: I'll go on my house call.

SOLNESS: Yes, do. But stop by later.

DR. HERDAL: *(playfully, looking at Hilde)* Wouldn't miss it for the world. Mr. Solness, you're a prophet after all.

SOLNESS: What do you mean?

DR. HERDAL: Youth did come knocking on your door.

SOLNESS: *(cheerfully)* Yes, but that was not what I meant.

DR. HERDAL: No. No, of course not. *(He leaves. Solness opens the right-hand door and calls into the room.)*

SOLNESS: Aline! Would you come in here, please? There's a Miss Wangel to see you.

MRS. SOLNESS: *(at door)* Who? *(sees Hilde)* My goodness! Is that you? *(goes over and takes her hand)* Well, well, you've finally come into town to see us.

SOLNESS: Miss Wangel has just arrived. She's wondering if we could put her up for the night.

MRS. SOLNESS: Stay with us? Of course! It would be a pleasure.

SOLNESS: She needs to get her clothes in order— that sort of thing.

MRS. SOLNESS: I'll do what I can. No more than my duty. Is your luggage on the way?

HILDE: I haven't any.

MRS. SOLNESS: Well, I'm sure we'll manage somehow. Now make yourself at home. I'll leave you to chat with my husband while I get a room ready for you.

33

SOLNESS: One of the nurseries. They're all ready, aren't they?

MRS. SOLNESS: Yes. There's more than enough room there. *(to Hilde)* Sit down and rest a bit. *(exits)*

(Hilde, hands behind her back, wanders around the room, looking at various things. Solness stands by the table, also hands behind his back. Watches her. Hilde stops and turns to him.)

HILDE: You have more than one nursery?

SOLNESS: We have three.

HILDE: Three! You must have lots of children.

SOLNESS: No. We have no children. You can be our child for tonight.

HILDE: For tonight. Yes. And I won't cry. I shall sleep like a log.

SOLNESS: I'm sure you're very tired.

HILDE: Not really. I shall sleep, though. I love to lie in bed—lie in bed and dream.

SOLNESS: Do you often dream at night?

HILDE: Oh yes. Almost every night.

SOLNESS: What do you dream about?

HILDE: Shan't tell. Not tonight. Some other time perhaps. *(wanders again, stops at the desk, touches the books and papers)*

(Solness crosses to her)

SOLNESS: You want something?

HILDE: No. I'm just looking around. Sorry. Perhaps I shouldn't.

SOLNESS: No. No. That's all right.

HILDE: Is that your writing? In the ledger there.

SOLNESS: No. That's my bookkeeper's.

HILDE: A woman?

SOLNESS: *(smiles)* Of course.

HILDE: She works for you.

SOLNESS: Yes.

HILDE: Is she married?

SOLNESS: No. She's single.

HILDE: I see.

SOLNESS: But she's getting married quite soon.

HILDE: That's nice—nice for her.

SOLNESS: But not so nice for me. I'll have no one to do my bookkeeping.

HILDE: I'm sure it wouldn't be very difficult to replace her.

SOLNESS: Perhaps you'd be interested in the position—mmm? You could be the one to write in the ledger.

HILDE: *(looking scornfully at him)* Wouldn't you like that! No thank you. None of that. *(Strolls across the room again. Sits in the rocking chair. Solness crosses to the table. Hilde continues in a raw tone.)* There are better things for me to do here than that. *(looks at him and smiles)* Wouldn't you agree?

SOLNESS: I suppose so. I'm sure you'll want to do some shopping. Buy yourself a smart outfit.

HILDE: *(amused)* No. I think I'll give that a miss.

SOLNESS: Oh?

HILDE: I haven't got any money.

SOLNESS: *(laughs)* No luggage. No money.

HILDE: Nothing. To hell with all that. I haven't a care in the world.

SOLNESS: I admire you for that.

HILDE: Only for that?

SOLNESS: There are other things. *(sits)* Is your father still alive?

HILDE: Still alive.

SOLNESS: You intend to do some studying here perhaps?

HILDE: No. No such intention.

SOLNESS: But you'll be staying for some time?

HILDE: Depends. *(She continues rocking, looking at him half seriously, half amusedly. She takes off her hat and puts it on the table.)* Mr. Solness?

SOLNESS: Yes?

HILDE: Do you have a good memory?

SOLNESS: Well. I . . . I think so.

HILDE: Then why don't you want to talk to me about what happened up there?

SOLNESS: *(startled)* At Lysanger? *(casually)* Well, there's not much to talk about, is there?

HILDE: *(looks at him reproachfully)* How can you say that?

SOLNESS: All right, then *you* talk to *me* about it.

HILDE: When the tower was finished the town held a big celebration. . . .

36

SOLNESS: Yes, that's one day I shall never forget.

HILDE: *(smiles)* Ah, won't you? That's nice of you.

SOLNESS: Nice?

HILDE: There was music in the churchyard. Hundreds and hundreds of people. We schoolgirls were all dressed in white. We all had little flags.

SOLNESS: Ah yes. The flags. I remember them.

HILDE: You climbed up the scaffolding. Right to the very top. You had a huge wreath. And you hung it up on the weathercock.

SOLNESS: *(interrupting her)* I used to do that years ago. It's an old custom.

HILDE: It was wonderful to stand down there and gaze up at you. So exciting. Think... if he should fall now. The great Master Builder himself.

SOLNESS: *(as though trying to change the subject)* Yes. Well, it just might have happened. One of those little monsters in white suddenly started waving violently at me and she was shouting—

HILDE: *(eyes ablaze)* "Hurrah for Mr. Solness! Three cheers for the Master Builder!" Yes!

SOLNESS: Waved her flag and flung it around so that I...I felt quite giddy watching it.

HILDE: *(quite serious)* That little monster was me.

SOLNESS: *(stares hard at her)* Of course. Of course it was you.

HILDE: *(joyously)* It was so exciting. So wonderful. I had never thought that there was a builder anywhere in the world who could build so high a tower. And then to see you. Standing there at

37

the very top. And you didn't feel giddy. That was what made me feel giddy.

SOLNESS: How were you so sure that I—

HILDE: Don't be silly. I knew it. I felt it in here. How else could you have stood up there—singing.

SOLNESS: *(astonished)* Singing? I was singing?

HILDE: Yes, you were.

SOLNESS: *(shaking his head)* I've never sung a note in my life.

HILDE: Well, you were singing then. It sounded like harps in the air.

SOLNESS: *(thoughtfully)* Most extraordinary.

HILDE: *(looks at him silently for a moment, then says softly)* It was afterwards...afterwards came the *real* thing.

SOLNESS: The real thing?

HILDE: Yes. Do I have to remind you of that too?

SOLNESS: Yes, a little. Remind me a little.

HILDE: They put on an enormous dinner in your honor at the club.

SOLNESS: Yes, yes, that evening. I left the following morning.

HILDE: When it was over, we invited you over to our house.

SOLNESS: I remember, Miss Wangel. You have a remarkable memory for details.

HILDE: Details! There you are again! I suppose it was just a detail that I was alone in the room when you came in.

SOLNESS: Were you?

HILDE: *(ignoring him)* I wasn't a little monster then.

SOLNESS: No. No, I'm sure.

HILDE: You said I looked lovely in my white dress. You said I looked like a princess.

SOLNESS: I'm sure that you did, Miss Wangel. And then feeling as I did that day so happy, so free—

HILDE: You said that when I grew up I could be your princess.

SOLNESS: *(short laugh)* Really? Is that what I said.

HILDE: Yes. That's what you said. And when I asked you how long I should wait, you said you'd come back in ten years, like a troll, and you'd carry me off—to Spain or somewhere. And you promised that you'd buy me a kingdom.

SOLNESS: *(as before)* Well, after a good dinner you don't spare any expense. But did I really say all that?

HILDE: *(softly laughing)* Yes. And you told me what we should call the kingdom.

SOLNESS: Oh, what?

HILDE: The kingdom of Orangia. That's what you said.

SOLNESS: A tasteful name.

HILDE: I didn't like it at all. I felt you were making fun of me.

SOLNESS: That was not my intention.

HILDE: No. Certainly not after what you did next—

SOLNESS: And what on earth did I do next?

HILDE: Well, this is really the limit! You've forgotten that too! How could anyone forget a thing like that.

SOLNESS: All right, just a hint... could you give me just a—

HILDE: (looking intently at him) You took me in your arms and you kissed me, Mr. Solness.

SOLNESS: I did? (getting up open-mouthed)

HILDE: Oh yes. You did. You held me in your arms. Both arms. You bent me backwards and you kissed me. Many times.

SOLNESS: But my dear Miss Wangel...

HILDE: (rising) You're not going to deny it?

SOLNESS: Yes. I am. I absolutely deny it.

HILDE: (looking scornfully at him) I see. (She turns and walks to the stove. Stands motionless, her back to him. Hands behind her back. Short pause.)

SOLNESS: (approaching her cautiously) Miss Wangel—? (Hilde is silent, motionless) Don't stand there like a statue. All these things you've been saying—you must have dreamed them. (puts his hand on her arm) Now listen to me— (Hilde removes her arm impatiently. Solness appears to think of something suddenly.) Wait a minute—no, there's more to it than this. (She is motionless. He speaks softly, determinedly.) I must have thought all this. Must have. I must have willed it, wished it, desired it. And no—isn't that it? Isn't that the explanation? (She is silent. He speaks impatiently.) All right! For God's sake, have your own way. I did—I did it.

40

HILDE: *(slight turn of the head, without looking at him)* You confess?

SOLNESS: Yes. Anything you say.

HILDE: You put your arms around me?

SOLNESS: Yes.

HILDE: And bent me over backwards?

SOLNESS: Yes. All the way backwards.

HILDE: And you kissed me?

SOLNESS: Yes. I kissed you.

HILDE: Many times?

SOLNESS: As many as you like.

HILDE: *(turning to face him, her eyes sparkling again)* There, you see. I got it out of you. Finally.

SOLNESS: *(with a wan smile)* How could I have forgotten something like that?

HILDE: *(sulking a little as she moves away from him)* You've kissed many women in your time, I'm sure.

SOLNESS: You mustn't think that of me.

(Hilde sits in the armchair. Solness leans on the rocking chair, watching her closely.)

SOLNESS: Miss Wangel?

HILDE: Yes.

SOLNESS: What happened after that? What happened between you and me?

HILDE: Nothing. You know that as well as I. The guests arrived and then— *(she gestures, a shrug)*

SOLNESS: Of course. The others came. I'm capable of forgetting that too.

HILDE: You haven't forgotten a thing. You're a little embarrassed. No one forgets something like that.

SOLNESS: No, I shouldn't think so.

HILDE: *(with the same sparkle)* Or perhaps you've forgotten what day it was?

SOLNESS: What day—?

HILDE: Yes, what day did you hang the wreath on the tower? Come on! Quick! Tell me.

SOLNESS: Hmm—I think I've forgotten the actual date—I know it was about ten years ago. Sometime in the fall.

HILDE: *(nodding her head slowly)* It was ten years ago. The 19th of September.

SOLNESS: Yes, that seems to be about right. What a memory you have. *(hesitates)* Wait a minute—today is September the 19th—

HILDE: Yes, it is. The ten years are up. And you didn't come for me—as promised.

SOLNESS: Promised? You mean threatened.

HILDE: I never took it as a threat.

SOLNESS: I was teasing you.

HILDE: Was that all it meant? Were you teasing me?

SOLNESS: I was just being playful. Look. I don't remember. But it must have been something like that. A bit of fun. You were only a child.

HILDE: Perhaps I wasn't such a child. Perhaps I wasn't such a little innocent as you thought.

SOLNESS: *(looking searchingly at her)* Did you really think that I would come back? Seriously?

HILDE: *(with a half-teasing smile)* Of course. That's exactly what I thought.

SOLNESS: That I'd come back to your house and carry you off with me?

HILDE: Just like a troll. Yes.

SOLNESS: And make you a princess?

HILDE: As you promised.

SOLNESS: And buy you a kingdom?

HILDE: *(gazing at the ceiling)* Why not? After all, it didn't have to be just an ordinary kingdom.

SOLNESS: But something just as good.

HILDE: Oh, at least just as good. *(glaring at him)* If you could build the highest church tower in the world—I was sure that you could come up with a kingdom. Some sort of kingdom.

SOLNESS: *(shaking his head)* I do not understand you, Miss Wangel.

HILDE: You don't? It's all so simple.

SOLNESS: I don't understand whether you mean what you say. Or whether you're making fun of me—

HILDE: Being playful? Teasing? A bit of fun? Me too?

SOLNESS: Exactly. Making fools of us both. *(looking at her)* How long have you known I was married?

HILDE: From the beginning. Why do you ask?

SOLNESS: *(casually)* Nothing. I just wondered. *(lowering his voice and looking at her directly)* Why did you come?

HILDE: I want my kingdom. Time's up.

SOLNESS: *(laughing in spite of himself)* You are the limit.

HILDE: *(laughing)* Give me my kingdom! Come on. Out with it. One kingdom. *(taps table)* Right away.

SOLNESS: *(pushing the rocking chair closer and sitting down)* I'm serious. Why did you come? What is it you want?

HILDE: For a start, I want to go around and look at everything you've built.

SOLNESS: That will take you some time.

HILDE: Yes. You've built so much.

SOLNESS: Indeed I have. Especially the last few years.

HILDE: Many more church spires too? Reaching to the skies?

SOLNESS: No. No, I don't build church spires any more. I don't build churches any more.

HILDE: What do you build then?

SOLNESS: Homes for people to live in.

HILDE: *(thinking)* You could put a tower—a small one—on top of them too, couldn't you?

SOLNESS: *(with a start)* What do you mean?

HILDE: I mean something tall, reaching, pointing up into the air. With a weathercock high up on the top. So high it makes you giddy.

44

SOLNESS: *(thoughtfully)* It's strange you should say that. That's something I still really want to do. Most of all.

HILDE: *(impatient)* Then why don't you do it?

SOLNESS: It's not what people want.

HILDE: How can they not want something like that?

SOLNESS: *(lightly)* I'm building a new house at the moment—right opposite here.

HILDE: For yourself.

SOLNESS: Yes. It's almost done. And it has a tower.

HILDE: A high one?

SOLNESS: Yes.

HILDE: Very high?

SOLNESS: Most people would think too high. At least for one's home.

HILDE: I shall take a look at it first thing in the morning.

SOLNESS: *(sitting with hand against his cheek)* Miss Wangel, tell me, what is your name—your Christian name?

HILDE: Don't you know?—Hilde.

SOLNESS: Hilde? Yes.

HILDE: You didn't remember? You called me Hilde once—that day when you misbehaved.

SOLNESS: I did?

HILDE: Yes. But you called me your "little Hilde." I didn't care for that.

SOLNESS: Ah, Miss Hilde, you didn't care for that.

45

HILDE: No. Not at that particular moment in my life. No. But Princess Hilde is going to suit me perfectly, I think.

SOLNESS: I don't doubt it. Princess Hilde of—what was the name of our kingdom?

HILDE: Sh! That was foolish and stupid and it's over. I want something different, something new.

SOLNESS: Isn't it strange—the more I think about it—I've spent all these years, these last ones searching in a kind of torment for—

HILDE: For what.

SOLNESS: Searching for something, some experience from a forgotten past. But I never could even remotely grasp what it might be.

HILDE: You should have tied a knot around your finger, Mr. Solness.

SOLNESS: I'd have forgotten why I tied it.

HILDE: The trolls of this world.

SOLNESS: I'm so glad that you've come to me.

HILDE: Are you?

SOLNESS: I've been so alone here—watching my life go by and feeling so utterly helpless. (*lowering his voice*) I should tell you—I've become afraid, very very afraid of the young.

HILDE: Pah! Young people are nothing to be afraid of.

SOLNESS: Oh yes, they are. That is why I have imprisoned myself. Locked myself in. But wait and see, youth will come in thunder, youth will break the lock of my door.

HILDE: Then it seems to me all you have to do is open the door and let the young enter.

SOLNESS: Open it?

HILDE: Yes. Let them come in. Let them be your friends.

SOLNESS: No, no, no. The younger generation—you see, they're punishment, retribution—the changing of the guard, as if they were marching under some new flag.

HILDE: *(rises trembling)* Can you find something for *me* to do, Mr. Solness?

SOLNESS: Of course. I have the feeling that you've come too—under this new flag. It's youth against youth.

(Dr. Herdal enters)

DR. HERDAL: So! You and Miss Wangel still here!

SOLNESS: Yes. We had a lot to talk about.

HILDE: Old things. New things.

DR. HERDAL: Oh, have you?

HILDE: It's been so much fun. Mr. Solness has an extraordinary memory. Remembers every little detail.

(Mrs. Solness enters)

MRS. SOLNESS: Miss Wangel? Your room's all ready.

HILDE: Oh, how kind of you.

SOLNESS: The nursery?

MRS. SOLNESS: Yes. The middle room. But we ought to have something to eat first, don't you think?

47

SOLNESS: *(nodding to Hilde)* So Hilde will sleep in the nursery.

MRS. SOLNESS: Hilde?

SOLNESS: Yes. Miss Wangel's name is Hilde. I met her when she was a child.

MRS. SOLNESS: Did you really, Halvard? Well, shall we go in? Supper's ready.

(She exits on Herdal's arm. Hilde picks up her hiking gear.)

HILDE: Is that true—what you said. *Can* you find a use for me?

SOLNESS: I have needed you more than anyone.

HILDE: *(hands clasped, happy)* Oh what a wonderful new world.

SOLNESS: *(tensely)* What?

HILDE: Then I have my kingdom.

SOLNESS: *(involuntarily)* Hilde!

HILDE: *(trembling)* Almost—that's all I meant.

ACT 2

Solness is sitting with Ragnar Brovik's portfolio in front of him. Occasionally he looks intently at a particular drawing. Mrs. Solness is watering the garden flowers. Solness occasionally watches her. She does not notice. Kaja Fosli enters.

SOLNESS: *(turns, casually)* Is that you?

KAJA: I just wanted to let you know that I was here.

SOLNESS: Good. Thank you. Is Ragnar there?

KAJA: No. Not yet. He was waiting for the doctor. But he'll be along soon to—

SOLNESS: How's the old man doing?

KAJA: Not very well. He's very sorry, but he can't leave his bed today.

SOLNESS: Of course not. Mustn't get up. But why don't you start your work.

KAJA: Yes. Will you want to speak to Ragnar when he comes in?

SOLNESS: No—I've got nothing to say to him in particular.

(Kaja exits; Solness sits)

MRS. SOLNESS: I shouldn't be surprised if he passes away—he too.

49

SOLNESS: He and who else?

MRS. SOLNESS: *(ignoring the question)* Yes. Brovik is going to die now too. Halvard, you wait and see.

SOLNESS: Aline, my dear, you could do with a little walk, I think.

MRS. SOLNESS: Yes, I suppose I could. *(continues watering the flowers)*

SOLNESS: Is she still asleep?

MRS. SOLNESS: Is it Miss Wangel you have on your mind— sitting there?

SOLNESS: *(casually)* I just happened to remember her.

MRS. SOLNESS: Miss Wangel's been up for hours.

SOLNESS: She has?

MRS. SOLNESS: When I looked in this morning she was busy arranging her things. *(at mirror, putting on hat)*

SOLNESS: *(pause)* So we finally did find a use for one of the nurseries.

MRS. SOLNESS: Yes. We did.

SOLNESS: And that's much better than them being up there empty.

MRS. SOLNESS: Yes. The emptiness, the horrible emptiness.

SOLNESS: *(rises, crosses)* Listen to me, Aline. Things are going to be better. You've got to see that. Much more pleasant. Life will be much easier— especially for you.

MRS. SOLNESS: From now on?

50

SOLNESS: Yes. Believe me, Aline—

MRS. SOLNESS: You mean, because *she's* come?

SOLNESS: No, of course not. I mean, once we're in the new house.

MRS. SOLNESS: *(putting on coat)* Do you think so, Halvard? Do you think that life will be better there?

SOLNESS: I'm sure of it. Don't you feel the same way?

MRS. SOLNESS: I have no feelings about the new house. No feelings at all.

SOLNESS: That is very painful for me to hear. It was for you, mostly, that I built it. *(helps her with coat)*

MRS. SOLNESS: *(stepping away from him)* You do too much for me as it is.

SOLNESS: Don't talk like that. I can't stand it when you say things like that.

MRS. SOLNESS: Then I won't say them.

SOLNESS: Look, I promise you that I'm right about this. Life will be better for you there. You'll see.

MRS. SOLNESS: Oh God. Better for me!

SOLNESS: Yes. Yes it will be. Believe that it will. Over there, there'll be so many things that will remind you of your old home.

MRS. SOLNESS: Mother's home. Father's home— which burned to the ground.

SOLNESS: Yes, my poor Aline. That was agony for you.

MRS. SOLNESS: *(breaks down)* Halvard, you can build and build and build—but you can never build me a real home again.

SOLNESS: *(crossing the room)* Then for God's sake let's not discuss it again.

MRS. SOLNESS: We don't normally ever discuss it. It is you who avoids the issue—

SOLNESS: *(looking at her)* Me? Why should I do that? Why should I avoid the issue?

MRS. SOLNESS: You think I don't know you, Halvard? You spend your life protecting me, finding excuses for me—all the time.

SOLNESS: For you! You can't be talking about yourself.

MRS. SOLNESS: Who else would I be talking about?

SOLNESS: *(to himself)* That too!

MRS. SOLNESS: What happened to the house—that was meant to be. I suppose there was disaster in the air—

SOLNESS: Yes, you're right. There was no way of stopping it—

MRS. SOLNESS: But it's what happened after the fire—that is the horror—that's in the—that...

SOLNESS: *(vehemently)* Put it out of your mind, Aline.

MRS. SOLNESS: How can I? What else is there to think about—to talk about, finally? For once I don't know how I can stand it any longer. And on top of everything, never to have the chance to find forgiveness for myself.

SOLNESS: For yourself!

MRS. SOLNESS: Yes. Forgiveness for myself. I had my duty to you and my duty to the children—to both sides. I should have been strong. I should have fought my fear. I should have fought my grief. Grief for my lost home. Oh, if I could have been strong. Halvard!

SOLNESS: *(softly, moved, coming closer)* Aline, you must promise me never to let those thoughts enter your mind again. Promise me now.

MRS. SOLNESS: God—promise, promise. Anyone can promise.

SOLNESS: *(clenched fists, crosses room)* This is impossible. Impossible. No sunlight on this darkness. Not a glimmer of light in our home.

MRS. SOLNESS: This is no home, Halvard.

SOLNESS: No. That is true. And God knows you may be right. Maybe it will be no better for us in the new house.

MRS. SOLNESS: It will never be better. It will always be empty—barren, just like here.

SOLNESS: Then why did we build it? Tell me. Why?

MRS. SOLNESS: You'll have to find the answers to that question inside yourself.

SOLNESS: And what do you mean by that, Aline?

MRS. SOLNESS: What do I mean?

SOLNESS: Yes. Damn it. You said it so strangely, as if there were other meanings behind your words.

MRS. SOLNESS: No. I can assure you—

SOLNESS: *(coming closer)* Oh come! I know what I know. I have eyes. I have ears. You can't fool me—

MRS. SOLNESS: What are you talking about? What are you trying to say?

SOLNESS: *(directly in front of her)* Isn't it true that you can find some secret, hidden meaning behind the most innocent thing that I might say?

MRS. SOLNESS: *I*? Are you suggesting that *I* do that?

SOLNESS: *(laughs)* It's perfectly natural—quite understandable when you're dealing with someone as sick as I am.

MRS. SOLNESS: Sick? Are you ill, Halvard?

SOLNESS: *(violently)* Half mad, then. A lunatic—anything that you want to call me.

MRS. SOLNESS: Halvard, for God's sake!

SOLNESS: But you're wrong. Both wrong. You and the doctor. That's not what's the matter with me. *(paces; Mrs. Solness watches)* In reality there is nothing whatever the matter with me.

MRS. SOLNESS: No. There's nothing wrong with you. But what is upsetting you so much?

SOLNESS: I feel sometimes that I will collapse under the weight of my debts—

MRS. SOLNESS: Debts? You don't owe a thing to anyone, Halvard.

SOLNESS: Yes, I do. I owe an incalculable debt to you, Aline—to you.

MRS. SOLNESS: What is all this about? You may as well tell me now.

SOLNESS: I have nothing to hide. I've never done you any harm—not that I was aware of. And yet I feel I will collapse under the weight of my guilt.

54

MRS. SOLNESS: Guilt towards me?

SOLNESS: Towards you more than anyone.

MRS. SOLNESS: Then you are—ill, after all, Halvard.

SOLNESS: Perhaps I am—perhaps so. *(door opens)* There are moments of rightness, however.

(Enter Hilde. She has made an alteration in her dress and let down her skirt.)

HILDE: Good morning, Mr. Solness.

SOLNESS: *(nodding)* Sleep well?

HILDE: Beautifully! Back to the cradle! I just lay there curled up like a princess.

SOLNESS: *(half smile)* Quite comfortable.

HILDE: Very.

SOLNESS: Did you dream last night?

HILDE: Yes, I did. But it was awful.

SOLNESS: How?

HILDE: Well, I dreamed that I was falling over a cliff, a precipice. Do you ever have that sort of dream?

SOLNESS: Yes, now and then—

HILDE: It's thrilling—to keep falling and falling.

SOLNESS: It makes my blood run cold.

HILDE: Do you pull your legs up under you as you're falling?

SOLNESS: Of course. As high as possible.

HILDE: Me too.

MRS. SOLNESS: *(taking her parasol)* I must go into town now, Halvard. *(to Hilde)* I'll try to pick up one or two things for you.

HILDE: *(putting arms around her)* Oh Mrs. Solness—you're such a dear. So kind. So very kind to me.

MRS. SOLNESS: *(freeing herself)* Far from it. It's only my duty. I'm very glad to do it.

HILDE: *(offended)* I don't see any reason why I couldn't go out myself—I've fixed my clothes. Why couldn't I.

MRS. SOLNESS: I think people would stare, my dear.

HILDE: Is that all? Let them. It's fun.

SOLNESS: *(suppressing anger)* Yes. But you see people might think that you were mad, too.

HILDE: Mad? Is the town full of mad people then?

SOLNESS: Here's one, at least. *(points to his forehead)*

HILDE: You, Mr. Solness?

MRS. SOLNESS: Oh Halvard, really!

SOLNESS: You hadn't noticed?

HILDE: No, of course not. *(laughs)* There's just one thing, though.

SOLNESS: There, you see, Aline.

MRS. SOLNESS: And what is that, Miss Wangel?

HILDE: I'm not saying.

SOLNESS: Please do.

HILDE: No thank you. *I'm* not so mad as that.

MRS. SOLNESS: When you and Miss Wangel are alone I'm sure she'll tell you, Halvard.

SOLNESS: You think she will?

MRS. SOLNESS: Yes. I'm sure she will. After all, you've known her so well, for such a long time. Ever since she was a child, remember? *(exits)*

HILDE: Does your wife dislike me very much?

SOLNESS: Is that what you thought?

HILDE: Didn't *you* think so?

SOLNESS: Aline has become very withdrawn in recent years, very shy with strangers.

HILDE: She has?

SOLNESS: If you could really get to know her though —she's so very nice—so kind and such a good heart.

HILDE: If that's what she's really like, then why did she say that thing about "duty"?

SOLNESS: Duty?

HILDE: She said she'd go and pick up some things for me because it was her *duty*. Duty. What a horrible, ugly little word.

SOLNESS: What do you mean?

HILDE: It's cold. Sharp. It jabs at you. Duty Duty Duty. You see. You feel it jabbing at you?

SOLNESS: I've never thought of it, really.

HILDE: Well, it does. And if she's so nice, why does she talk like that?

SOLNESS: But, Good Lord, what is she supposed to say?

HILDE: Well, she could have said she'd do it because—because she liked me a lot. Something like that. She could have said something warm, pleasant.

SOLNESS: That's what you'd have liked?

HILDE: Yes. That's all. *(wanders, looks at books)*

HILDE: You have a lot of books.

SOLNESS: It's a good collection.

HILDE: Have you read them all?

SOLNESS: I need to try to. And you. Do you read much?

HILDE: No. Never really. I just stopped. It all seemed so irrelevant.

SOLNESS: My feelings too.

(Hilde crosses to table and portfolio)

HILDE: Did you draw these?

SOLNESS: No. They were done by a young man who helps me out here.

HILDE: A student of yours?

SOLNESS: Well, yes. I've taught him a few things.

HILDE: He must be very clever. *(sits)* He is, isn't he?

SOLNESS: Not bad. Not bad. For *my* purposes, however—

HILDE: Oh, I'm sure he's very clever indeed.

SOLNESS: You think you see that in the drawings?

HILDE: Pah! These are mere scribbles. But if *you've* been teaching him—

SOLNESS: Well, as far as that goes—there are lots of people who have studied under me, and they've gotten nowhere.

58

HILDE: *(looks, shakes her head)* I can't, for the life of me—I can't understand how you can be so stupid.

SOLNESS: Stupid? Is that what you think of me?

HILDE: Yes. I do. If you can spend your time teaching these people when—

SOLNESS: Why shouldn't I?

HILDE: Mr. Solness, why should you? What's the good of it? Only you should be allowed to build, to create. You should be unique, alone, above all others. Now you know.

SOLNESS: Hilde!

HILDE: Well?

SOLNESS: And where did all that come from?

HILDE: Was I wrong? Very wrong?

SOLNESS: No, no. That's not what I mean. Let me tell you something.

HILDE: Yes.

SOLNESS: That is the very same thought that obsesses me—when I sit here in my solitude, in my silence.

HILDE: That seems perfectly natural.

SOLNESS: Perhaps you'd already noticed that?

HILDE: No, not really.

SOLNESS: But just now when you said—when you thought I was—let's say unbalanced. There was one thing you said—

HILDE: I was thinking of something quite different.

SOLNESS: What was that?

59

HILDE: I'm not going to tell you.

SOLNESS: *(crosses room)* Well—well—as you wish. *(at window)* Come here and I'll show you something.

HILDE: What is it?

SOLNESS: You see over there, in the garden?

HILDE: Yes?

SOLNESS: Right above that large quarry—

HILDE: That new house, you mean?

SOLNESS: The one that's being built, yes. Almost finished.

HILDE: It has a very high tower.

SOLNESS: The scaffolding's still up.

HILDE: Is that your new house?

SOLNESS: Yes.

HILDE: Are there nurseries in the new house too?

SOLNESS: Three. Same as here.

HILDE: And no child.

SOLNESS: And there never will be one.

HILDE: *(half smiling)* Isn't that exactly what I said—

SOLNESS: That—?

HILDE: That is one way you are a little mad.

SOLNESS: Was that what you were thinking of?

HILDE: I was thinking of the empty nurseries— where I slept.

SOLNESS: We did have children once, Aline and I.

HILDE: You did?

SOLNESS: Two little boys the same age.

HILDE: Twins?

SOLNESS: Yes, twins. They'd be eleven or twelve now.

HILDE: So—both of them? You lost them both?

SOLNESS: They were with us for about three weeks. Perhaps not even that— *(passionately)* Oh Hilde, I can't tell you how good it's for me that you've come. I have someone to talk to. At last.

HILDE: Can't you talk to—*her* too?

SOLNESS: No. Not about this. Not as I want to talk—need to talk. And not about many other things, either.

HILDE: *(quietly)* Was that all you meant when you said you needed me.

SOLNESS: Principally yes. At least that's what I meant yesterday. Today I'm not so sure. Come and sit down with me, Hilde. Sit on the sofa—so that you can look into the garden. Would you care to hear?

HILDE: Yes, I love listening to you.

SOLNESS: Then I'll tell you about it.

HILDE: Now I can see the garden and I can see you. Please begin.

SOLNESS: Out there on the hill where you see the new house—

HILDE: Yes.

SOLNESS: That's where Aline and I lived for the first years of our married life. There was an old house up there that belonged to her mother. We inherited it. There was an enormous garden.

61

HILDE: And a tower?

SOLNESS: No. No towers. Nothing like that one. From the outside it looked like a big dark ugly wooden box. On the inside it was comfortable enough. Cozy even.

HILDE: Did you tear the old thing down?

SOLNESS: No, it burned down.

HILDE: The whole house?

SOLNESS: Yes.

HILDE: Was that a great loss to you?

SOLNESS: That depends. As a builder, in many ways it made me.

HILDE: Well, but—?

SOLNESS: It was just after the birth of the boys.

HILDE: The twins, yes.

SOLNESS: They were so healthy, so chubby when they were born. And in such a short time, day by day, you could see them growing.

HILDE: Little babies grow quickly.

SOLNESS: It was the most wonderful thing in the world to see Aline lying there with the two of them in her arms—then there was the fire.

HILDE: What happened? Tell me! Was anyone caught in the fire?

SOLNESS: No. Everyone got out safely—

HILDE: So what happened?

SOLNESS: Aline had been thoroughly terrified. The alarm—the escape—the frenzied desperation—

the ice-cold night air—they had to be carried out just where they lay—she and the babies.

HILDE: Was it too much for them?

SOLNESS: Oh no, they were fine. But Aline contracted a fever. Her milk was affected. Still, she insisted on nursing them herself. It was her duty, she said. Anyway, both of them, both of our little boys— *(clenches fists)* oh, oh—

HILDE: *That* was too much for them.

SOLNESS: *That* was too much for them. That was how we lost them.

HILDE: It must have been terribly hard for you.

SOLNESS: Yes, it was, but ten times harder for Aline— Oh, why do such things have to happen here on this earth! From the day I lost them I never wanted to build another church. Never.

HILDE: What about in our town? Didn't you like building the church tower?

SOLNESS: No. I did not like it. I remember the relief I felt when it was over.

HILDE: I remember.

SOLNESS: And now I shall never build anything like that again. No churches, no church towers.

HILDE: Only houses for people to live in.

SOLNESS: Houses for human beings, Hilde.

HILDE: But houses with high towers and spires.

SOLNESS: If possible. *(in a lighter tone)* Anyway, as I said, that fire made me. As a builder, I mean.

HILDE: Why don't you call yourself an architect, as others do?

SOLNESS: I didn't have enough of a formal educa-
tion in the field. Most of what I know, I've
taught myself.

HILDE: That has not stopped you.

SOLNESS: No. Thanks to the fire. You see, I took
that enormous garden, landscaped it into private lots for villas, and I was able to follow my
own creative instincts. I reached the top very
quickly.

HILDE: Then you must be very happy—this is the
life you have made.

SOLNESS: Happy? You say that too—like all the rest
of them?

HILDE: Yes. I should say you must be happy. All
that's wrong is that the children prey on your
mind.

SOLNESS: The twins—it's not so easy to forget, Hilde.

HILDE: *(uncertainly)* They bother you so much, still,
after all these years?

SOLNESS: *(looking at her steadily)* A happy man, you
said—

HILDE: Yes. Aren't you—I mean, apart from that?

SOLNESS: When I told you about the fire—

HILDE: Yes?

SOLNESS: Didn't you notice something significant,
something special?

HILDE: No. Was there something?

SOLNESS: *(quietly)* It was through that fire, that fire
alone, that I gained the chance to build those
homes for human beings. Cozy, comfortable,

64

sunlit homes where fathers and mothers and hosts of children can live in comfort and happiness. Where they can know the meaning of the joy of living in this world. Where they can belong one to another, share the big things, the little things of life.

HILDE: Well, isn't there happiness for you in being able to build such beautiful homes?

SOLNESS: But the price, Hilde. The terrible price I had to pay.

HILDE: Can you never get over that?

SOLNESS: No. In order to build homes for others I have to give—give up forever the home that might have been my own. I mean, a home for lots of children, for a mother and a father too.

HILDE: (cautiously) But did you have to give it up—forever?

SOLNESS: (nods slowly) That was the price I paid for my so-called happiness. My happiness—it couldn't be bought for less.

HILDE: But it might all work out—surely?

SOLNESS: Never. Not in this world. That's another consequence of the fire—and of Aline's illness afterwards.

HILDE: (looking at him carefully) And yet you built the nurseries.

SOLNESS: (seriously) Have you ever noticed, Hilde, how the impossible always whispers in your ear?

HILDE: The impossible?—oh yes. You've known that too?

SOLNESS: Yes.

HILDE: Then there is in you that troll quality we talked about.

SOLNESS: Why a troll?

HILDE: What would you call it, then?

SOLNESS: *(rising)* Yes, yes, could be. *(angry)* But why shouldn't the troll be in me?—when things always seem to turn out as they do for me! Always!

HILDE: What do you mean?

SOLNESS: Listen to me carefully, Hilde. All my achievements, everything I've built or created— all the beauty, the security, the comfort—the magnificence perhaps, all this—God, I can't bear to think of it.

HILDE: What's so awful?

SOLNESS: All this has to be paid for. Not with money but with human happiness. Not my own alone—with others too. Hilde, try to understand. That's the price of my reputation as an artist. That's what I have paid. And so have others. And I have to watch it being paid, here, daily, again and again, eternally.

HILDE: Now you're thinking of her?

SOLNESS: Yes, mostly of Aline. Because she had a life too just as I have mine. She had a vocation. But hers had to be crushed so that mine could flourish. Hers was cut down, smothered, crushed. You see, she had a talent for building too.

HILDE: She? For building?

SOLNESS: Not houses or towers or spires—not the things I build.

66

HILDE: What, then.

SOLNESS: *(gently, with feeling)* She could build a soul within a child. She could teach them to become brave and strong, beautiful, complete. She could teach them to become full human beings, honorable human beings. That was her talent. And now it lies buried—unused, useless. Eternally. And for no reason on earth. Her talent lies like rubble and ashes.

HILDE: Yes—but even if this is true...

SOLNESS: It is true! It is. I know it's true.

HILDE: But all the same, it's not your fault.

SOLNESS: *(looking at her closely)* That's the terrible question—that's the ugly question—that gnaws at my mind day and night.

HILDE: But why?

SOLNESS: Think of it this way—suppose it *was* my fault, in some sense.

HILDE: You mean the fire?

SOLNESS: I mean everything—the fire, everything. And yet at the same time *not* my fault—totally innocent at the same time.

HILDE: Mr. Solness, when you talk like that—I feel that perhaps you are ill, after all.

SOLNESS: I don't think there will ever be sanity over that question.

(Ragnar opens the door cautiously. Hilde crosses the room.)

RAGNAR: *(seeing Hilde)* Oh, excuse me. Mr. Solness. *(starts to leave)*

67

SOLNESS: No, no. Don't leave. Let's get it over and done with.

RAGNAR: Yes. I hope we can.

SOLNESS: Your father's no better, I hear.

RAGNAR: No, he's failing fast, I'm afraid. And that's why I beg you—please give me some indication, some favorable response to one or two of the drawings—for my father to see before he—

SOLNESS: Leave your drawings out of this.

RAGNAR: Have you looked at them?

SOLNESS: Yes, I have.

RAGNAR: And they're worthless? No doubt I'm worthless too?

SOLNESS: *(not answering)* You are to stay on here—working for me. Everything will work out well for you. You'll marry Kaja and life will be easy for you—happy even. Just drop the issue of your own building.

RAGNAR: And I should go home and tell my father, is that it? As I promised. Is that what you want me to tell him before he dies?

SOLNESS: Tell him—tell him what you like, I don't care. Why tell him anything? *(suddenly)* There's nothing I can do about it, Ragnar.

RAGNAR: May I have the drawings to take with me?

SOLNESS: Yes, take them. Take them by all means. They're on the table.

RAGNAR: Thank you.

HILDE: No—leave them there.

SOLNESS: What for?

HILDE: Because I want to look at them too.

SOLNESS: But I thought you had—well, just leave them then.

RAGNAR: As you wish.

SOLNESS: And now—go home to your father.

RAGNAR: Yes. I must.

SOLNESS: Ragnar, don't ask me to do things over which I have no control. Do you hear me? Don't ask again.

RAGNAR: No. No. Excuse me— *(bows and exits; Hilde sits)*

HILDE: *(angry)* That was a cruel thing to do.

SOLNESS: Is that what you think too?

HILDE: Yes. It was terribly cruel. A mean and ugly thing to do.

SOLNESS: You don't understand my position.

HILDE: That doesn't matter—you shouldn't be like that.

SOLNESS: You said yourself, just now, that no one else but me should have the right to build.

HILDE: I may have the right to say such things, but you certainly don't.

SOLNESS: On the contrary, considering how dearly I have paid for the right.

HILDE: Yes, your precious domestic comfort, I suppose you mean.

SOLNESS: Yes—and my peace of mind. Don't forget that.

HILDE: *(rising)* Peace of mind! Yes. I see. I do understand—Poor Master Builder. You feel that—

SOLNESS: *(laughing)* Just sit down again a moment, Hilde, and I'll tell you something funny.

HILDE: Well?

SOLNESS: This will sound ridiculous, but this whole story started with a little crack in a chimney.

HILDE: A crack in a chimney?

SOLNESS: Yes, that's what started it. *(moves closer, sits)*

HILDE: Well, tell me about this crack in the chimney.

SOLNESS: I had noticed a small split in some bricks in the flue. This was long before the fire. Every time I went up to the attic, I always took a look at it—to see if it was still there.

HILDE: And was it?

SOLNESS: Yes. No one else had noticed it.

HILDE: And you said nothing?

SOLNESS: Not a word.

HILDE: And you didn't think of repairing it?

SOLNESS: Actually, I did. I thought about it but didn't do anything. Every time I decided to work on it—it was as if a hand was holding me back. All right, I thought, if not today, tomorrow. So it never got done.

HILDE: But why did you keep putting it off?

SOLNESS: I was becoming obsessed by an idea— *(slowly, quiet)* I began to believe that through that crack I might emerge and force my way upon the world as a master builder.

HILDE: *(looking straight ahead)* That must have been thrilling.

SOLNESS: It was. Almost irresistible—totally irresistible. At the time it all seemed so simple. It was going to happen, as I saw it, sometime before midday. We were to be out, Aline and I, driving in the sleigh. The servants were to be at home and they would have lit a huge fire in the stove.

HILDE: Because it was such a bitterly cold day?

SOLNESS: Freezing. Yes. And they wanted the house to be warm and cozy for Aline when she came home.

HILDE: She hates the cold?

SOLNESS: She does. Then, as we drove home we were supposed to see the smoke.

HILDE: Just the smoke?

SOLNESS: That's all at first. But by the time we reached the gate, that ugly old wooden box was to be a mass of flames. That's the way I wanted it to be.

HILDE: If only that had been what happened!

SOLNESS: You may well say that, Hilde.

HILDE: But just a moment, Mr. Solness—how can you be sure the fire started in the crack in the chimney?

SOLNESS: I'm not sure. Not at all. In fact, I'm certain it wasn't the cause at all.

HILDE: What?

SOLNESS: It was proven—and there is no doubt about this—that the fire broke out in a clothes closet. In an entirely different part of the house.

71

HILDE: Then what's the point of your story—your obsession with the crack in the chimney.

SOLNESS: Will you let me explain, Hilde?

HILDE: Certainly, but try to make some sense.

SOLNESS: I'll try. *(moves chair)*

HILDE: Please go on, Mr. Solness.

SOLNESS: *(confidingly)* I believe—and something tells me that you do too—I believe that there are certain people, chosen people, who have the gift, the ability, the power to wish for something, *desire* it, to *will* something—and to do this so insistently, so inexorably that in the end the outcome is inevitable. Don't you believe that?

HILDE: *(inscrutably)* If that is true, then perhaps one day we shall find that *I* am one of the chosen.

SOLNESS: But it's not by one's own power alone that these things come to be. We must always depend on the "helpers and the servers" if we are to succeed. But they never come by themselves. They too have to be summoned, insistently, inexorably—willed from within oneself.

HILDE: Who are these helpers and servers?

SOLNESS: Let's talk about that some other time.... For the moment, let's concentrate on the fire and its cause.

HILDE: Don't you think it would have happened despite all this—I mean, even if you hadn't wished for it?

SOLNESS: If the house had belonged to the old man, say, Knut Brovik—it would never have burned down so conveniently for *him*. I'm sure of that. He doesn't know how to summon the helpers—

72

or the servers, for that matter. *(rises)* So you see, Hilde, it *is* my fault. It's my fault that two little lives were lost. And perhaps it's my fault that Aline never became what she could and should have become—what she most longed to be.

HILDE: No. What about the so-called helpers and servers? Is it not their fault?

SOLNESS: Who summoned them? *I* did. And they came. And they obeyed my will. *(more excited)* *That's* what all these well-meaning people call having luck on your side. But let me tell you how it feels to have that sort of luck. It feels as though here above my heart the flesh is open, raw. And all the helpers and servers keep on stripping pieces of skin off other people to close the wound. But the wound never heals—never. Oh, if you only knew how it throbs and burns.

HILDE: *(looking attentively)* You *are* ill, Mr. Solness. Very ill, I think.

SOLNESS: Why not call it madness—that is what you mean.

HILDE: No, it's not a question of sanity. It has nothing to do with your mind.

SOLNESS: Then what is it? Tell me.

HILDE: I wonder whether you weren't born with a weak conscience?

SOLNESS: A weak conscience—what in God's name do you mean by that?

HILDE: That your conscience is delicate, fragile. As if it didn't have the strength to grapple with things, to lift and bear the heavy burdens of life.

SOLNESS: And what sort of conscience *should* one have?

73

HILDE: I would like your conscience to be strong.

SOLNESS: Ah. Strong. Do you have such a conscience?

HILDE: Yes, I think I do. I've never noticed the contrary.

SOLNESS: Perhaps it's never been truly tested.

HILDE: It was not easy to leave my father. I adore my father.

SOLNESS: Oh come, just for a month or two—

HILDE: No. I don't think I shall ever go home again.

SOLNESS: Never? Then why did you leave him?

HILDE: *(half serious)* Have you forgotten that the ten years are up?

SOLNESS: Oh nonsense. Was anything wrong at home?

HILDE: No. There was something within me that drove me, goaded me to come here. It had a kind of softness and allure in its call to me.

SOLNESS: That's exactly it. That's it, Hilde. There's a troll in you too. In me, in you. In us. Don't you see—that's what summons the powers out there. And then we *have* to give in. We have no choice.

HILDE: I half believe you're right, Mr. Solness.

SOLNESS: *(pacing)* Oh Hilde, there are demons on the loose in the world, unseen demons.

HILDE: Demons too?

SOLNESS: Good demons, bad demons. Fair-haired demons, black-haired demons. If only we knew

74

which ones possessed us. It would be so easy then.

HILDE: Or if your conscience were truly strong, healthy, brimming with health—then you could do anything you wanted.

SOLNESS: I think most of the people in this world are as weak as I am.

HILDE: Probably.

SOLNESS: *(leaning against the table)* In the sagas—did you ever read the old sagas?

HILDE: Oh yes. When I used to read—

SOLNESS: In the sagas you read about the Vikings who sailed to other countries and plundered and pillaged and killed the men.

HILDE: And captured the women.

SOLNESS: Carried them off.

HILDE: Took them home in their ships.

SOLNESS: Treated them like savag—like demon trolls.

HILDE: *(half-closed eyes)* I think that must have been thrilling.

SOLNESS: Carrying off the women?

HILDE: Being carried off.

SOLNESS: *(looking at her)* I see.

HILDE: What are you getting at, Mr. Solness—I mean, with the Vikings.

SOLNESS: There's your strong conscience right there —in those men. They got back home. They ate. They drank. They laughed like children. The

75

women too. Most of those women very soon became inseparable from the men. Couldn't give them up. Does that make sense to you, Hilde?

HILDE: *They* make perfect sense. The women.

SOLNESS: Ah—perhaps you could do the same?

HILDE: Why not?

SOLNESS: Live by choice with a barbarian like that?

HILDE: If I loved him.

SOLNESS: But could you love a barbarian?

HILDE: My God, you don't *plan* these things.

SOLNESS: No—it's the trolls inside again.

HILDE: Yes, and the devils—your friends. Fair and dark.

SOLNESS: *(warm)* Then I'll ask them to choose kindly for you, Hilde.

HILDE: They have already. For now and forever.

SOLNESS: Hilde, at times you're like a wild creature, a wild bird of the woods.

HILDE: Hardly, I don't hide in the undergrowth.

SOLNESS: No. No. You're more like a bird of prey.

HILDE: Yes. Much more, perhaps—and why shouldn't I be? Why shouldn't I go hunting too? Seize my prey? All I want is to set my claws deep and have my own way.

SOLNESS: Hilde, do you know what you are?

HILDE: A strange kind of bird.

SOLNESS: No. You're like the dawn. When I look at you it's as if I were looking at the sunrise.

HILDE: Tell me, Mr. Solness, are you sure you've never called for me—summoned me—within yourself, I mean.

SOLNESS: *(slowly, softly)* I sometimes think I must have.

HILDE: What did you want with me?

SOLNESS: You, Hilde, are youth.

HILDE: *(smiles)* The youth that terrifies you?

SOLNESS: Yes. And that I hunger for, deep within me.

HILDE: *(rises, goes to Ragnar's portfolio, holding it out)* About these drawings.

SOLNESS: Put them away. I've seen enough of them.

HILDE: You must write your comments on them.

SOLNESS: I will not do so. Never.

HILDE: But the old man is near death. One small kindness to him, to his son before they're parted forever. And perhaps later he could build his building—from those drawings.

SOLNESS: That's exactly what he would do. That's his plan, that's the upstart's plan.

HILDE: But, my God, if that's all—what's a small lie?

SOLNESS: A lie! Hilde, take those damn drawings away from me.

HILDE: *(slightly withdrawing)* All right. All right. No need to snap at me like that. Talk about trolls. That's just how you're behaving—where's pen and ink?

SOLNESS: There are none.

HILDE: Perhaps in the other room, where that girl works?

SOLNESS: Hilde, stay here. You suggested that I could lie a little. Well, perhaps for the old man's sake I could bring myself to do it. I destroyed him, broke him.

HILDE: Him too?

SOLNESS: I had to have room for myself. But Ragnar—he must never be allowed to get ahead.

HILDE: I pity him. Anyway, there's not much hope—you said he has no talent.

SOLNESS: If Ragnar Brovik gets the chance, he'll break *me*, destroy *me* as I did his father.

HILDE: Break you! You think he has the power to do that?

SOLNESS: Yes. He has. *He* is the younger generation working to break down my door, to destroy Solness the Master Builder.

HILDE: (*reproachfully*) And you want to keep him out? For shame, Mr. Solness.

SOLNESS: My struggle has cost me my life's blood. And I'm afraid—I'm afraid that the helpers and servers will no longer hear my calls.

HILDE: Then you'll just have to make do without them.

SOLNESS: It's hopeless, Hilde. Change is coming. Maybe it'll be soon, maybe later. But the retribution is inexorable.

HILDE: (*frightened*) Don't say those things. You want to kill me? Do you want to take away from me what means more to me than life itself?

78

SOLNESS: What is that?

HILDE: The need to see you in all your greatness. To see you with a wreath in your hand, high up, high high up on a church tower. *(calm again)* So—get your pencil out. Do you have a pencil in your pocket?

SOLNESS: *(takes one out)* Here we are.

HILDE: *(puts portfolio down)* Good. Let's sit here, the two of us—*(he sits, she stands)* and we'll write on the drawings something very nice, very complimentary, for this dreadful Ragvar—whatever his name is.

SOLNESS: *(writes, turns)* Tell me one thing, Hilde.

HILDE: Yes.

SOLNESS: If you've really been waiting for me these ten years—

HILDE: Then what?

SOLNESS: Why didn't you write to me? I could have answered you.

HILDE: No, no, no. That's exactly what I did *not* want.

SOLNESS: Why not?

HILDE: I was afraid that everything would be ruined. ...But we must write on the drawings, Mr. Solness.

SOLNESS: Yes, of course.

HILDE: *(leaning forward)* Something kind. From the heart—oh how I hate this Ra—ga—

SOLNESS: *(writing)* Have you never really loved anyone, Hilde?

HILDE: *(harshly)* What? What did you say?

SOLNESS: Have you ever been in love, I said.

HILDE: With anyone else, I suppose you mean?

SOLNESS: *(looks at her)* With anyone else. Yes. Never? In all these ten years, never?

HILDE: Oh yes. Once or twice. When I was furious with you for not coming.

SOLNESS: Then you *have* cared for other people too?

HILDE: A little, perhaps. For a week or so. Good heavens, Master Builder, you must know all about things like that.

SOLNESS: Why have you come here?

HILDE: Stop talking. Hurry up. The poor old man might die any minute.

SOLNESS: Answer me, Hilde. What do you want of me?

HILDE: I want my kingdom.

SOLNESS: Hmm— *(he glances rapidly at the door and goes on writing; Mrs. Solness enters with packages)*

MRS. SOLNESS; I've brought a few of the things myself. The rest will be sent on later.

HILDE: You're really much too kind.

MRS. SOLNESS: My simple duty—that's all.

SOLNESS: *(reading over)* Aline?

MRS. SOLNESS: Yes, Halvard.

SOLNESS: Did you happen to notice whether she— whether the bookkeeper was out there?

MRS. SOLNESS: Of course she's out there. She is at her desk, as she always is when *I* go through the room.

SOLNESS: *(puts the drawing in the portfolio)* Then I'll just give her these and tell her that—

HILDE: *(takes the portfolio)* Oh, let me have the pleasure of doing that! *(goes to door, turns)* What's her name?

SOLNESS: Miss Fosli.

HILDE: No. No. That sounds so formal. Her first name?

SOLNESS: Kaja, I believe.

HILDE: *(opens door)* Kaja. Quick. Come in here. The Master Builder wants to talk to you. *(Kaja appears)*

KAJA: *(looking in alarm)* You wanted me—

HILDE: *(holding out the portfolio)* Take these home, Kaja. The Master Builder has written his comments on them now.

KAJA: Oh, at last.

SOLNESS: Give them to the old man to look at as soon as possible.

KAJA: I'll go at once—

SOLNESS: Yes, do—now Ragnar has his chance to do some building.

KAJA: Can he stop by and thank you for all you've—

SOLNESS: I want no thanks. Tell him that from me.

KAJA: Yes. I will.

SOLNESS: And you can tell him that I will no longer need his services—nor yours, either.

KAJA: *(softly)* Nor mine, either?

SOLNESS: You'll have other things on your mind now—lots of arrangements to make. That's as it should be. Take the drawings home now, Miss Fosli. At once, do you hear?

KAJA: Yes, Mr. Solness.

MRS. SOLNESS: What deceitful eyes she has—

SOLNESS: Her? She's just a fool.

MRS. SOLNESS: I see what I see, Halvard. You're really letting them go?

SOLNESS: Yes.

MRS. SOLNESS: Her as well?

SOLNESS: Isn't that what you wanted?

MRS. SOLNESS: But to get rid of her! Ah, well. I'm sure you have someone to fall back on, Halvard.

HILDE: *(playfully)* Well, I'd be no good behind a desk.

SOLNESS: Never mind, never mind, Aline. Everything will be all right. You just think about getting ready to move into the new home—as soon as possible. This evening we'll hang up the wreath— *(to Hilde)* at the very top of the tower. What do you say to that, Miss Hilde?

HILDE: It will be wonderful to see you up there again—high up.

SOLNESS: Me!

MRS. SOLNESS: Whatever put that idea into your head, Miss Wangel? My husband! It's impossible—he gets so dizzy.

SOLNESS: Dizzy? Not at all.

82

MRS. SOLNESS: Oh yes. I assure you.

HILDE: But I saw him myself—right at the top of a high church tower.

MRS. SOLNESS: Yes, people still talk about that—but it's impossible.

SOLNESS: Impossible. Impossible. But all the same, I stood there.

MRS. SOLNESS: Halvard, how can you say that? You can't even bear standing on the balcony—two stories high. You've always been afraid.

SOLNESS: Perhaps you'll see something quite different this evening.

MRS. SOLNESS: *(terrified)* No, no, no. I hope to God that's something I never see. I'm going to call for the doctor at once. He'll know how to stop you.

SOLNESS: Aline!

MRS. SOLNESS: Halvard! You know you're ill. This proves it. God, oh God. *(she exits)*

HILDE: *Is* it true or isn't it?

SOLNESS: That I get dizzy?

HILDE: That my Master Builder *dare* not, *cannot* climb as high as he can build?

SOLNESS: Is that how you look at it?

HILDE: Yes.

SOLNESS: Is there no part of me that I can keep my own, safe from you?

HILDE: *(looking to window)* Up there, then. Right up there!

SOLNESS: *(crossing to her)* You could live there, Hilde. In the uppermost room of the tower. You could live there like a princess.

HILDE: *(ambiguously, half seriously)* That's what you promised—

SOLNESS: Is it?

HILDE: You said I was to be a princess—that you'd give me a kingdom. Then you went and—

SOLNESS: What makes you think you're not in some kind of dream, some kind of fantasy that's taken hold of you?

HILDE: *(scornfully)* You mean that you didn't do it?

SOLNESS: I hardly know, myself. But one thing I know for certain—I—

HILDE: You what? Go on.

SOLNESS: I ought to have done it.

HILDE: *(animatedly)* You could never be dizzy.

SOLNESS: So, we'll hang the wreath this evening, my princess. Princess Hilde.

HILDE: *(wryly)* Over your new home. Yes.

SOLNESS: Over the new house—that will never be a home for me. *(exits)*

HILDE: *(through whispered words we hear)* —terribly thrilling!

ACT 3

Mrs. Solness in a white crepe shawl sits in the arm-chair. Hilde enters, wearing a hat. On her blouse is a bouquet of wild flowers.

MRS. SOLNESS: You've been for a walk around the garden, Miss Wangel?

HILDE: Yes. I've been exploring it—

MRS. SOLNESS: And found some flowers too, I see.

HILDE: There are hundreds of them—in among the barley.

MRS. SOLNESS: Fancy that! Are there really? Still? I so rarely go out there.

HILDE: *(crossing to her)* Really? Don't you? I'd have thought you'd have trotted down there every day.

MRS. SOLNESS: I don't trot anywhere—not anywhere —not any longer, Miss Wangel.

HILDE: But you must go down there sometimes. It's such a beautiful garden.

MRS. SOLNESS: It all seems so—so alien to me. I'm almost afraid to go and see it again.

HILDE: Your own garden?

MRS. SOLNESS: It doesn't feel like mine anymore.

HILDE: What do you mean?

MRS. SOLNESS: No. It is no longer mine, Miss Wangel. Things were so different when my mother and father were alive. But they've done such terrible things to the garden. They've divided it up into lots, and they've built houses for so many people—people I don't know. They just sit in their windows and stare at me.

HILDE: Mrs. Solness?

MRS. SOLNESS: Yes?

HILDE: Would you mind if I stayed with you here for awhile?

MRS. SOLNESS: Of course not. I'd be delighted—if you'd like to.

HILDE: *(puts stool by chairs)* It's so wonderful to sit in the sun, warming yourself like a cat.

MRS. SOLNESS: *(puts hand on back of Hilde's head)* It's kind of you to want to be with me. I thought you were going to join my husband.

HILDE: Why should I want to join him?

MRS. SOLNESS: I thought perhaps you were helping him with something.

HILDE: No. Anyway, he's not at home at the moment. He's with the workers—down there. He seemed to be in such a terrible mood. I didn't dare say a word to him.

MRS. SOLNESS: You know, underneath all that he's very kind and very gentle.

HILDE: Kind and gentle, Mrs. Solness?

MRS. SOLNESS: You don't really know him yet, Miss Wangel.

HILDE: *(affectionately)* Are you pleased to be moving into your new house?

MRS. SOLNESS: I suppose I should be pleased. It's what Halvard wants—

HILDE: Oh, I don't mean *that*.

MRS. SOLNESS: Oh yes, Miss Wangel, that's important. It's my duty to try to please him. But there are times when it's so hard—so hard to *make* oneself obey.

HILDE: Yes. That must be very hard.

MRS. SOLNESS: It is. Especially when one has as many faults as I do—

HILDE: Especially when one has gone through as much as you have—

MRS. SOLNESS: How do you know about that?

HILDE: Your husband told me.

MRS. SOLNESS: He rarely talks to me about it. Yes, I have had more than my share of trouble in this life, Miss Wangel.

HILDE: *(sympathetically)* Poor Mrs. Solness. First there was the fire—

MRS. SOLNESS: I lost everything. Everything that was mine.

HILDE: And what happened after—that was even worse.

MRS. SOLNESS: *(looks at her)* Worse?

HILDE: The worst thing of all.

MRS. SOLNESS: What do you mean?

HILDE: When you lost the two little boys.

MRS. SOLNESS: Oh yes, the boys. No, you see that was something quite different. That was the will of God. And one can only submit to that will in such things. Submit and give thanks.

HILDE: And can you give thanks?

MRS. SOLNESS: Not always, I regret to say. I know well enough that it's my duty—but at times I cannot.

HILDE: I think that's only natural.

MRS. SOLNESS: And very often I have to remind myself that it was a just punishment for me.

HILDE: Why?

MRS. SOLNESS: Because I hadn't the strength to bear my misfortune.

HILDE: But I don't see how the—

MRS. SOLNESS: Oh no no, Miss Wangel—don't talk to me anymore about the two little boys. We should feel nothing but joy when we think of them. For, you see, they are so happy—so happy now. No, it's the *small* losses in life that cut one to the heart—the loss of all little things, things that might seem insignificant to other people.

HILDE: *(touches Mrs. Solness's knee affectionately)* Dear Mrs. Solness, what sort of things do you mean?

MRS. SOLNESS: Just the little things, as I said. All the old portraits we had on the walls were burned. And all the old silk dresses—which we'd had in the family for generations and generations. And we had a collection of antique lace that belonged to mother and grandmother—that was burnt too. And the jewels! *(sadly)* And then all the dolls.

HILDE: The dolls?

MRS. SOLNESS: *(choking back tears)* I had nine beautiful dolls.

HILDE: They were burned too?

MRS. SOLNESS: All of them. Oh, it was hard—so hard for me.

HILDE: There were dolls that you'd kept? I mean stored away? Dolls that you'd played with as a little girl?

MRS. SOLNESS: They were not stored away. The dolls and I had gone on living together.

HILDE: After you had grown up?

MRS. SOLNESS: Yes, long after that.

HILDE: After you were married?

MRS. SOLNESS: Oh yes. As long as he knew nothing about it, it was—but they were all burned. All of them, poor things. No one thought of saving them. I can't bear to think of it. So tragic. You mustn't laugh at me, Miss Wangel.

HILDE: I'm not laughing. Not at all.

MRS. SOLNESS: In a way, you see, there was life in them too. I carried them under my heart. Like little unborn children.

(Dr. Herdal, hat in hand, enters and observes the two of them)

DR. HERDAL: Well, Mrs. Solness, catching a cold by the window?

MRS. SOLNESS: *(rises)* Yes. There's something I must talk to you about.

DR. HERDAL: Certainly. Shall we go into the other room? *(to Hilde)* Still dressed for mountain climbing, Miss Wangel?

HILDE: *(happily rising)* Yes, in full uniform. But no climbing today—no breaking my neck. You and I will sit down here quietly and watch.

DR. HERDAL: What are we to look at?

MRS. SOLNESS: *(in alarm)* Hush. Hush! For God's sake. He's coming. Please get the idea out of his head. And let us be friends, Miss Wangel. I'm sure we could be, aren't you?

HILDE: *(throws arms around her)* Oh, if only we could.

MRS. SOLNESS: *(disengages herself)* There, there! Here he comes, doctor. Let me have a word with you.

DR. HERDAL: Do you want to talk about him?

MRS. SOLNESS: You can be sure it's about him. So come in.

(They exit. Solness enters. Hilde is serious.)

SOLNESS: *(notices the door closing)* Hilde, have you noticed that as soon as I come in she leaves?

HILDE: I've noticed that as soon as you come in, you *make* her leave.

SOLNESS: Perhaps. But that's not my fault. *(looks)* Are you cold, Hilde? You look as if you are.

HILDE: I've just come out of a tomb.

SOLNESS: What do you mean by that?

HILDE: I've been chilled to the bone, Mr. Solness.

SOLNESS: I think I understand—

HILDE: Why did you come up here?

SOLNESS: I caught sight of you from over there.

HILDE: Then you must have seen her too.

SOLNESS: I knew she would leave once I came.

HILDE: Is that very painful for you—does it hurt you when she avoids you?

SOLNESS: In a way, but it's also a relief.

HILDE: To have her out of your sight?

SOLNESS: Yes.

HILDE: So that you don't have to see how heavily the loss of the two little boys weighs upon her?

SOLNESS: That's the main reason.

(Hilde looks out over the garden)

SOLNESS: Did you have a long talk with her?

(Hilde still silent)

SOLNESS: A long talk—I asked?

(still silent)

SOLNESS: What did she talk about, Hilde? Poor Aline—the little boys, I suppose.

(Hilde shudders and nods)

SOLNESS: She will never get over it. Never. *(crosses)* You're standing there like a statue again. Just like last night.

HILDE: *(turns to him)* I am going away.

SOLNESS: Going away?

HILDE: Yes.

SOLNESS: No. I won't let you.

HILDE: What is there for me to do here?

SOLNESS: Simply to *be* here, Hilde.

HILDE: *(looks at him)* Yes, I'm sure. You know it wouldn't stop there.

SOLNESS: *(recklessly)* So much the better!

HILDE: *(vehemently)* I can't do any harm to someone I *know*. I can't take anything that belongs to her.

SOLNESS: Whoever said you *would*?

HILDE: A stranger, yes! That's quite a different thing. Someone I'd never laid eyes on. But someone I've come close to— No. No. Never. I couldn't do it. No.

SOLNESS: I never proposed that you should.

HILDE: Oh, Mr. Solness, you know very well what would happen if I stayed. That is why I'm going away.

SOLNESS: What's going to happen to me when you're gone? What shall I have to live for then? After you've gone.

HILDE: *(an indefinable look in her eyes)* It will not be hard for *you*. You have your duty to her. Live for that duty.

SOLNESS: Too late. The powers—the—the—

HILDE: —the demons—

SOLNESS: Yes—the demons. And the troll within me as well. They have drained the lifeblood out of her. *(laughs)* And they did it for my *happiness*. Yes. Yes. *(sadly)* And she has died—died for my sake. And I live my life chained to her corpse. *(in anguish)* I—I who cannot live without joy in my life. *(sits on bench)*

HILDE: What will you build next?

SOLNESS: I don't believe I shall build much more, Hilde.

HILDE: No warm comfortable homes—for a mother and a father and a host of children?

SOLNESS: I wonder whether there will be any use for such homes in the future?

HILDE: Poor Mr. Solness. You have dedicated your life to that idea for the past ten years.

SOLNESS: That is correct.

HILDE: *(in an outburst)* It's all so absurd. So utterly senseless.

SOLNESS: All what?

HILDE: Not to be able to seize your own happiness—to control your own life. And all because someone you *know* happens to stand in the way.

SOLNESS: Someone you cannot set aside.

HILDE: I wonder. I wonder if that really *is* true. Perhaps after all one *does* have the right. And yet—somehow—oh to be able to sleep it all away. *(puts her head and arm on the table, closes her eyes)*

SOLNESS: *(turns the chair and sits)* Did you live in a warm, comfortable home up there with your father?

HILDE: *(not moving)* I lived in a cage.

SOLNESS: And you really don't want to go back there?

HILDE: Wild birds can't live in cages.

SOLNESS: They must be free to hunt—free as the air.

HILDE: Birds of prey were meant to hunt.

SOLNESS: If only one had the Viking spirit in one's life.

HILDE: *(opens her eyes)* And the other thing? Say what that was!

SOLNESS: A strong conscience.

(Hilde sits, eyes sparkling)

HILDE: I know what you're going to build next, Master Builder.

SOLNESS: Then you know more than I do, Hilde.

HILDE: Yes. Master Builders are not very intelligent.

SOLNESS: Well, what's it going to be?

HILDE: The castle.

SOLNESS: What castle?

HILDE: My castle, of course.

SOLNESS: Now you want a castle?

HILDE: You owe me a kingdom, don't you?

SOLNESS: That's what you *say*.

HILDE: All right. You owe me the kingdom. And you can't have a kingdom without a castle. That I'm sure of.

SOLNESS: *(more animated)* No. They usually go together.

HILDE: Very well. Then build it for me at once.

SOLNESS: *(laughs)* Must you have it this instant?

HILDE: Of course. The ten years are up. And I'm not going to wait any longer. So—out with my castle, Master Builder.

SOLNESS: It's not easy to owe you anything, Hilde.

HILDE: You should have thought of that before. It's too late now. So— *(taps the table)* the castle on the table! It's my castle. I want it at once!

SOLNESS: *(leans forward seriously)* What sort of castle do you have in mind? What does it look like?

HILDE: *(seeming to go inward)* My castle stands on a high hill—at a great height—with a clear view on all sides—so that I can see far—far around.

SOLNESS: Of course it has a high tower?

HILDE: A tremendously high tower. And at the very top of the tower there will be a balcony. And I will stand on it—

SOLNESS: *(clutches his forehead)* How could you enjoy standing at such a dizzy height?

HILDE: It's what I want. And I will do it. I will stand and look down on the rest of the world—on the people who are building churches, building homes for mothers and fathers and hosts of children. And you may come up and look out with me.

SOLNESS: Is the builder to be allowed to stand beside the princess?

HILDE: If the builder *will*.

SOLNESS: Then I think the builder will be there.

HILDE: The builder will be there.

SOLNESS: But he'll never build again. Poor builder.

HILDE: Oh yes he will. We will work together. The two of us. And we shall build the most beautiful —the most utterly beautiful thing in all the world.

95

SOLNESS: Hilde, tell me what that is.

HILDE: *(smiles, speaks as if to a child)* Builders are so very stupid. No intelligence.

SOLNESS: No doubt that's true. But tell me what it is, this utterly beautiful thing. What is it that we shall build together?

HILDE: Castles in the air.

SOLNESS: Castles in the air?

HILDE: Yes. Do you know what a castle in the air is?

SOLNESS: Something utterly beautiful, according to you.

HILDE: *(rising)* Yes. Of course. Castles in the air. They're so easy to escape to. And so easy to build. Especially for the builders who have a—a dizzy conscience.

SOLNESS: *(rises)* From now on we shall build together, Hilde. The two of us.

HILDE: A real castle in the air?

SOLNESS: Yes. One built on a solid foundation.

(Ragnar Brovik enters carrying a wreath)

HILDE: The wreath! Oh, it will be wonderful.

SOLNESS: *(surprised)* Why have you brought the wreath, Ragnar?

RAGNAR: I promised the foreman I would.

SOLNESS: *(relieved)* Then your father is better, I hope.

RAGNAR: No.

SOLNESS: Did what I wrote cheer him up?

RAGNAR: It came too late.

SOLNESS: Too late!

RAGNAR: When she brought it he was unconscious. He had had a stroke.

SOLNESS: Then you must go home and be with him. You must look after your father.

RAGNAR: He doesn't need me now.

SOLNESS: But you ought to be with him. Surely.

RAGNAR: She is at his bedside.

SOLNESS: Kaja.

RAGNAR: *(looking darkly at him)* Yes. Kaja.

SOLNESS: Go home, Ragnar. Be with him and her. Give me the wreath.

RAGNAR: You don't mean that you're going to—

SOLNESS: I'll take it down to the men. *(takes it)* You go on home. We don't need you here today.

RAGNAR: No. I dare say you don't need me. But today I'm going to stay.

SOLNESS: Very well. As you like.

HILDE: I'm going to stand here and watch you, Master Builder.

SOLNESS: *Watch* me.

HILDE: It will be terribly thrilling.

SOLNESS: We'll discuss it later. *(exits)*

HILDE: *(to Ragnar)* I think you might at least have thanked him.

RAGNAR: Thanked him? You think I ought to thank him.

HILDE: Yes, I do.

RAGNAR: I think perhaps I ought to have thanked you.

HILDE: Why so?

RAGNAR: But you must be careful, Hilde Wangel— you don't really know him yet.

HILDE: I know him better than anyone.

RAGNAR: *(laughs)* Thank him! Do you realize that he's kept me here for years? No advancement. My own father had no confidence in me. I had no confidence in myself. All because of him. He kept me here just because he wanted—

HILDE: What did he want?

RAGNAR: He wanted to keep her with him.

HILDE: The girl at the desk?

RAGNAR: Yes.

HILDE: That is not true! You're telling lies.

RAGNAR: I wouldn't have believed it either. Until today. She told me herself, everything.

HILDE: What do you mean, "everything." What did she say? Tell me. At once!

RAGNAR: She said she had emptied her mind of everything but him. He was her total obsession. She could think of nothing else. She said she could never leave him—that she will remain here, to be near him.

HILDE: She won't be allowed to.

RAGNAR: *(hesitant)* Who will stop her?

HILDE: You think he will let her stay?

RAGNAR: No. No. I think I understand what has happened now. After all this she would be merely in the way.

HILDE: You understand nothing. Nothing. Not if you talk like that. No. I will tell you why he kept her here.

RAGNAR: Yes, tell me.

HILDE: He needed you.

RAGNAR: Is that what he told you?

HILDE: No, but that's the truth. I *know* it is. It must be. It has to be the reason.

RAGNAR: The moment you arrived, he let her go.

HILDE: He let *you* go. It was you. He doesn't care about women like her.

RAGNAR: Is it possible that he's been afraid of me all this time?

HILDE: Afraid? Don't be so conceited.

RAGNAR: He must have seen something in me. And seen it a long time ago, too. Anyway he's a coward—yes, you'll see.

HILDE: Oh yes, I'm sure.

RAGNAR: Yes, I'm right. He *is* a coward—he is. The great Master Builder. He's not afraid of depriving others of any happiness in life. That's what he did to my father. And to me. But in fact if he had to climb that little bit of scaffolding out there—he'd do anything rather than that.

HILDE: You should have seen him as I once saw him. High high up. Dizzyingly high.

RAGNAR: You were there?

HILDE: Yes, I saw him. He looked so proud, so free as he stood there at the top and put the wreath on the weather vane.

RAGNAR: I knew he had done that—tried it once in his life, one solitary time. It's still a tradition for us younger men. But for him, no power on earth would make him do it again.

HILDE: He will do it again today.

RAGNAR: I'm sure he will!

HILDE: We shall see.

RAGNAR: That is something that neither you nor I will see.

HILDE: I *will* see it. I will and *must* see it.

RAGNAR: He won't do it. He is too afraid. It's a terror that he cannot conquer—Master Builder though he be.

(Mrs. Solness enters)

MRS. SOLNESS: Isn't he here? Do you know where he is?

RAGNAR: Mr. Solness is down with the men.

HILDE: He took the wreath with him.

MRS. SOLNESS: Took the wreath! Oh God. My God—Brovik, you must go down there, make him come back.

RAGNAR: Shall I tell him you wish to speak to him, Mrs. Solness?

MRS. SOLNESS: Yes. No. No—don't tell him that I want anything! Tell him—he should come at once.

RAGNAR: Very well. I will do so, Mrs. Solness. *(exits)*

MRS. SOLNESS: Oh Miss Wangel, I'm so desperately worried. You've no idea.

HILDE: What is there to be so afraid of?

MRS. SOLNESS: Surely you can understand? Think if he were to try it. If he were to decide to climb the scaffolding. . . .

HILDE: Do you think he will?

MRS. SOLNESS: You never know what he might decide to do. I'm afraid there's nothing he mightn't think of doing.

HILDE: Perhaps you too think that he's—well . . .

MRS. SOLNESS: I don't know what to think anymore. The doctor has been telling me some things that—well— And then when I think of some of the things he's told me—

(*Dr. Herdal enters*)

DR. HERDAL: Is he coming?

MRS. SOLNESS: Yes, I think so. I've sent for him, anyway.

DR. HERDAL: I think you should go back to your room.

MRS. SOLNESS: Oh no. No. I must stay here and wait for Halvard.

DR. HERDAL: You have some visitors, some ladies in the hallway.

MRS. SOLNESS: Now? How inconvenient.

DR. HERDAL: They said they had to see the ceremony.

MRS. SOLNESS: I suppose I'd better go. It's my duty.

HILDE: Why not ask them to leave?

MRS. SOLNESS: That would never do. Now that they're here, it's my duty to see them. Please stay here and wait for Halvard.

DR. HERDAL: And keep him busy for as long as possible—

MRS. SOLNESS: Yes. Please do. Miss Wangel—don't let go of him.

HILDE: Wouldn't it be better for you to do that?

MRS. SOLNESS: Yes, God knows it's my duty to. But one has so many duties.

DR. HERDAL: I can see him coming.

MRS. SOLNESS: And I have to go!

DR. HERDAL: *(to Hilde)* Don't tell him I'm here.

HILDE: I won't. I'm sure I'll find something else to talk about.

MRS. SOLNESS: Don't let go of him. I believe you can do that best. *(they exit)*

SOLNESS: You? I was afraid it was Aline or the doctor.

HILDE: What were you afraid of? You're easily frightened.

SOLNESS: Do you think so?

HILDE: Yes. People say that you're afraid to climb the scaffolding.

SOLNESS: That's very different.

HILDE: Then it's true? You are afraid?

SOLNESS: Yes I am.

HILDE: Afraid of falling, getting killed?

SOLNESS: No, not that.

HILDE: Of what, then?

SOLNESS: Afraid of punishment, retribution, Hilde.

HILDE: Retribution? I don't understand.

SOLNESS: Sit down and I'll tell you something.

HILDE: Please, tell me.

SOLNESS: You know that I began my career by building churches—

HILDE: Yes. Yes.

SOLNESS: I believe I can say in all honesty that I built those poor little churches with such a sense of devotion—a devotion that was warm and came from the heart. So—

HILDE: What?

SOLNESS: Well, I think He ought to have been pleased with me.

HILDE: He? Whom do you mean?

SOLNESS: He whose churches they were, of course. He to whose honor and glory they were dedicated.

HILDE: Yes, but what makes you so sure that He wasn't pleased with you?

SOLNESS: He! *He* pleased with *me*! How can you even think that, Hilde? He who put the troll in my soul—to dominate my life. He who ordered them to serve me, day and night—all—all the...

HILDE: Demons.

SOLNESS: Yes, of both kinds. No, he has shown me, in so many ways, that he wasn't pleased with me. That was why he made the house burn down.

HILDE: That was why?

SOLNESS: Yes. Don't you understand? He wanted to give me the opportunity of becoming a great master in my field—he wanted me to build more and more churches. At first I didn't understand what he was doing. Then one day I understood. It came to me in a flash.

HILDE: When was that?

SOLNESS: When I was building the church tower up at Lysanger.

HILDE: I thought so.

SOLNESS: You see, Hilde, up there everything was new and different. I used to take a walk and think deeply, within myself. Then I understood why he had taken the children from me. It was, quite simply, so that there should be no other hold over me. No love, no happiness, nothing. I was to be a Master Builder—nothing else. I was to dedicate my life to building for him. *(laughs)* But nothing came of that, of course.

HILDE: What did you do then?

SOLNESS: At first I searched—I searched my own soul.

HILDE: And then?

SOLNESS: And then it happened. I did the impossible. I no less than He. I had never before been able to climb up to a great height—to be free. But that day I did it.

HILDE: Yes, yes you did.

SOLNESS: When I stood there, high up, overlooking everything, and when I was hanging the wreath over the vane, I spoke to Him. I said, Hear me now Almighty one. Henceforth I shall be free. I in my universe. Thou in Thine. I will never build any more churches for Thee—I shall build homes for human beings.

HILDE: *That* was the music I heard in the air.

SOLNESS: But in time, His turn came.

HILDE: What do you mean?

SOLNESS: Building homes for human beings is not worth a penny, Hilde.

HILDE: You say that now?

SOLNESS: Yes. Because now I see it. Men have no use for these homes—homes to be happy in. And I should have had no use for such a home. If I'd had one. *(bitter laugh)* You see, that's the whole point. That's been at the core of things ever since I remember—*nothing* was ever truly built, *nothing* was ever truly *sacrificed* for the chance to build. Nothing. Nothing. All is nothing.

HILDE: Then will you never build anything else?

SOLNESS: On the contrary, I'm ready to begin.

HILDE: What then? What will you build? Tell me.

SOLNESS: I believe there's only one possible place for human beings to live and be happy. That's what I'm going to build.

HILDE: Mr. Solness—you mean our castle in the air?

SOLNESS: The castle in the air—yes.

HILDE: I'm afraid you would be dizzy before we got halfway up.

SOLNESS: Not if we could climb together, Hilde, hand in hand.

HILDE: Together with me? Alone? Wouldn't there be others?

SOLNESS: Who could there be?

HILDE: Oh, the girl at the desk—Kaja. Don't you want to bring her along too?

SOLNESS: Ah, is that what Aline was talking to you about?

HILDE: Is it true—yes or no?

SOLNESS: I will not answer such a question. You must believe in me—totally, completely.

HILDE: For ten years I have believed in you—without question, without question.

SOLNESS: You must go on believing in me.

HILDE: Then let me see you again standing free—up there, on high.

SOLNESS: Oh Hilde, I could do that once, not anymore.

HILDE: I will have you do it. I will, just once more, Mr. Solness—do the impossible, once more.

SOLNESS: If I try it, Hilde, I will stand up there and speak to Him as I did before.

HILDE: What will you say to Him?

SOLNESS: I will say to Him, Hear me Almighty Lord. Thou may'st judge me as seems best unto Thee. Henceforth I will build nothing but the most beautiful thing in the world—

HILDE: Yes. Yes.

SOLNESS: Build it with a princess, whom I love—

HILDE: Yes, tell Him that. Tell Him that.

SOLNESS: Yes. And then I will say to Him, Now I shall go down and throw my arms around her and kiss her—

HILDE: Many times! Say that!

SOLNESS: Many many times, I will say.

HILDE: And then—?

SOLNESS: Then I will wave my hat, and descend to earth—and I will do what I promised Him.

HILDE: *(arms outstretched)* Now I see you again as I did when I heard music in the air!

SOLNESS: What made you what you are, Hilde?

HILDE: How did you make me what I am?

SOLNESS: The princess shall have her castle.

HILDE: Oh, Mr. Solness. My castle, my beautiful castle. Our castle in the air.

SOLNESS: Built upon a solid foundation.

(Crowd of people, music of wind instruments. Mrs. Solness in fur, Dr. Herdal carrying her white shawl. Ragnar enters from the garden.)

SOLNESS: Is there to be music?

RAGNAR: Yes, it's the band from the Masons' Union. *(to Solness)* The foreman asked me to tell you that he's ready to go up with the wreath.

SOLNESS: All right. I'll go down and see him.

MRS. SOLNESS: Why? What do you need to go down there for?

SOLNESS: I must be with the men, down below.

MRS. SOLNESS: Yes. But stay below, with them.

SOLNESS: That's where I always stand—except on special occasions. *(exits)*

MRS. SOLNESS: *(calling after)* Tell the foreman to be careful when he goes up. Promise me, Halvard. *(he goes)*

DR. HERDAL: You see, I was right—he's not thinking of doing anything foolish.

MRS. SOLNESS: What a relief! Two workmen have fallen, you know. Both killed on the spot. *(to Hilde)* Thank you, Miss Wangel, for keeping such a firm hold on him. I would never have succeeded.

DR. HERDAL: Yes, Miss Wangel, you know how to keep a firm grip on a man—when you set your mind to it.

(Ragnar comes to her)

RAGNAR: *(half whispers)* Miss Wangel, do you see that crowd of young men down in the street?

HILDE: Yes.

RAGNAR: They're fellow students of mine—they've come to see the Master.

HILDE: Why? What do they want to see?

RAGNAR: They want to see that he hasn't got the courage to climb to the top of his own house.

HILDE: Ah, that's what they want, is it?

RAGNAR: He's kept us all down for so long, that man. Now we'll watch him kept down himself.

HILDE: You won't see that, not this time.

RAGNAR: *(smiles)* No? Then where will he be?

HILDE: High up. Up by the weather vane. That's where you'll see him.

RAGNAR: Him? I'll believe it when I see it.

HILDE: He has the will to reach the top—and that is where you'll see him.

RAGNAR: The will, yes. Yes, I'm sure. But he simply cannot do it. His head would be spinning— before he was halfway up. He'd have to crawl down again on his hands and knees.

DR. HERDAL: There goes the foreman up the first ladders.

MRS. SOLNESS: He's got the wreath to carry. I hope he'll be careful.

RAGNAR: That's not the foreman. It's—

HILDE: It's the Master Builder.

MRS. SOLNESS: It's Halvard. Oh my God, Halvard! Halvard!

DR. HERDAL: Shhh. Don't shout at him.

MRS. SOLNESS: I must go to him! He must come down!

DR. HERDAL: Don't move. Any of you. Not a sound!

HILDE: He climbs and he climbs—higher and higher. Higher and higher. Look! Just look!

RAGNAR: He must turn back. He can't possibly go on.

HILDE: Up and up. He'll reach the top soon.

MRS. SOLNESS: I shall die—God, I'm so afraid. I can't bear to watch.

DR. HERDAL: Then don't look at him.

HILDE: There, he's reached the planks at the top. Right at the top.

DR. HERDAL: Nobody move, do you hear?

HILDE: At last. At last! Now I see him again. Free and proud, again.

RAGNAR: This is imposs—

HILDE: This is how I have seen him all these ten years. Look how steadily he stands there. But terribly thrilling all the same. Look at him. Now he's putting the wreath on the weather vane.

RAGNAR: I feel as if I were watching something— impossible.

HILDE: Yes. That's right. The impossible—that's what he's doing right now. Can you see anyone up there with him?

RAGNAR: There's no one else.

HILDE: Yes. There's someone. Someone he has to fight with.

RAGNAR: No. You are mistaken.

HILDE: Then you hear no music in the air, either?

RAGNAR: It's just the wind in the trees.

HILDE: I hear music, a beautiful powerful music. *(shouts)* Look...Look. Now he's waving his hat. He's waving to us, us down here. Oh, wave back—wave back to him! It is finished now. *(tears the shawl from the doctor and waves it)* Hurrah! Hurrah for the Master Builder!

DR. HERDAL: Stop, stop for God's sake!

(Crowd waves, cries hurrah. Sudden silence. Shrieks. Body falls.)

MRS. SOLNESS AND OTHERS: He's fallen! He's falling! He's fallen!

(Mrs. Solness falls backwards. Confusion. Dr. Herdal rushes out. Silence.)

HILDE: My Master Builder.

RAGNAR: He must be crushed to pieces—killed on the spot.

A VOICE: The doctor—call the doctor.

RAGNAR: I can't move—

A VOICE: Then call down to him—

RAGNAR: How is he? Is he alive?

A VOICE: The Master Builder is dead.

OTHER VOICES: His skull is broken—he fell into the stone quarry.

HILDE: *(turns to Ragnar)* I can't see him up there any longer.

RAGNAR: God, how terrible. He couldn't do it. He couldn't do it.

HILDE: He climbed to the very top. And I heard harps in the air. My—my Master Builder.

ELEPHANT PAPERBACKS

American History and American Studies
Stephen Vincent Benét, *John Brown's Body,* EL10
Henry W. Berger, ed., *A William Appleman Williams Reader,*
    EL126
Andrew Bergman, *We're in the Money,* EL124
Paul Boyer, ed., *Reagan as President,* EL117
Robert V. Bruce, *1877: Year of Violence,* EL102
George Dangerfield, *The Era of Good Feelings,* EL110
Clarence Darrow, *Verdicts Out of Court,* EL2
Floyd Dell, *Intellectual Vagabondage,* EL13
Elisha P. Douglass, *Rebels and Democrats,* EL108
Theodore Draper, *The Roots of American Communism,* EL105
Joseph Epstein, *Ambition,* EL7
Paul W. Glad, *McKinley, Bryan, and the People,* EL119
Daniel Horowitz, *The Morality of Spending,* EL122
Kenneth T. Jackson, *The Ku Klux Klan in the City, 1915–1930,*
    EL123
Edward Chase Kirkland, *Dream and Thought in the Business
    Community, 1860–1900,* EL114
Herbert S Klein, *Slavery in the Americas,* EL103
Aileen S. Kraditor, *Means and Ends in American Abolitionism,*
    EL111
Leonard W. Levy, *Jefferson and Civil Liberties: The Darker Side,*
    EL107
Seymour J. Mandelbaum, *Boss Tweed's New York,* EL112
Thomas J. McCormick, *China Market,* EL115
Walter Millis, *The Martial Spirit,* EL104
Nicolaus Mills, ed., *Culture in an Age of Money,* EL302
Nicolaus Mills, *Like a Holy Crusade,* EL129
Roderick Nash, *The Nervous Generation,* EL113
William L. O'Neill, ed., *Echoes of Revolt: The Masses,
    1911–1917,* EL5
Glenn Porter and Harold C. Livesay, *Merchants and
    Manufacturers,* EL106
Edward Reynolds, *Stand the Storm,* EL128
Geoffrey S. Smith, *To Save a Nation,* EL125
Bernard Sternsher, ed., *Hitting Home: The Great Depression in
    Town and Country,* EL109
Athan Theoharis, *From the Secret Files of J. Edgar Hoover,* EL127
Nicholas von Hoffman, *We Are the People Our Parents Warned
    Us Against,* EL301
Norman Ware, *The Industrial Worker, 1840–1860,* EL116
Tom Wicker, *JFK and LBJ: The Influence of Personality upon
    Politics,* EL120
Robert H. Wiebe, *Businessmen and Reform,* EL101
T. Harry Williams, *McClellan, Sherman and Grant,* EL121
Miles Wolff, *Lunch at the 5 & 10,* EL118
Randall B. Woods and Howard Jones, *Dawning of the Cold
    War,* EL130

European and World History
Mark Frankland, *The Patriots' Revolution,* EL201
Ronnie S. Landau, *The Nazi Holocaust,* EL203
Clive Ponting, *1940: Myth and Reality,* EL202

ELEPHANT PAPERBACKS

Theatre and Drama

Robert Brustein, *Reimagining American Theatre,* EL410
Robert Brustein, *The Theatre of Revolt,* EL407
Irina and Igor Levin, *Working on the Play and the Role,* EL411
Plays for Performance:
    Aristophanes, *Lysistrata,* EL405
    Anton Chekhov, *The Seagull,* EL407
    Fyodor Dostoevsky, *Crime and Punishment,* EL416
    Georges Feydeau, *Paradise Hotel,* EL403
    Henrik Ibsen, *Ghosts,* EL401
    Henrik Ibsen, *Hedda Gabler,* EL413
    Henrik Ibsen, *The Master Builder,* EL417
    Henrik Ibsen, *When We Dead Awaken,* EL408
    Heinrich von Kleist, *The Prince of Homburg,* EL402
    Christopher Marlowe, *Doctor Faustus,* EL404
    The Mysteries: Creation, EL412
    The Mysteries: The Passion, EL414
    Sophocles, *Electra,* EL415
    August Strindberg, *The Father,* EL406

Literature and Letters

Stephen Vincent Benét, *John Brown's Body,* EL10
Isaiah Berlin, *The Hedgehog and the Fox,* EL21
Philip Callow, *Son and Lover: The Young D. H. Lawrence,* EL14
James Gould Cozzens, *Castaway,* EL6
James Gould Cozzens, *Men and Brethren,* EL3
Clarence Darrow, *Verdicts Out of Court,* EL2
Floyd Dell, *Intellectual Vagabondage,* EL13
Theodore Dreiser, *Best Short Stories,* EL1
Joseph Epstein, *Ambition,* EL7
André Gide, *Madeleine,* EL8
John Gross, *The Rise and Fall of the Man of Letters,* EL18
Irving Howe, *William Faulkner,* EL15
Aldous Huxley, *After Many a Summer Dies the Swan,* EL20
Aldous Huxley, *Ape and Essence,* EL19
Aldous Huxley, *Collected Short Stories,* EL17
Sinclair Lewis, *Selected Short Stories,* EL9
William L. O'Neill, ed., *Echoes of Revolt: The Masses,*
    1911–1917, EL5
Ramón J. Sender, *Seven Red Sundays,* EL11
Wilfrid Sheed, *Office Politics,* EL4
Tess Slesinger, *On Being Told That Her Second Husband Has*
    Taken His First Lover, and Other Stories, EL12
B. Traven, *The Carreta,* EL25
B. Traven, *Government,* EL23
B. Traven, *March to the Montería,* EL26
B. Traven, *The Night Visitor and Other Stories,* EL24
Rex Warner, *The Aerodrome,* EL22
Thomas Wolfe, *The Hills Beyond,* EL16